Aiming for Progress in Writing and Grammar

Book 3

Second Edition

William Collins' dream of knowledge for all began with the publication of his first book in 1819. A self-educated mill worker, he not only enriched millions of lives, but also founded a flourishing publishing house. Today, staying true to this spirit, Collins books are packed with inspiration, innovation and practical expertise. They place you at the centre of a world of possibility and give you exactly what you need to explore it.

Collins. Freedom to teach.

Published by Collins
An imprint of HarperCollins*Publishers*
77–85 Fulham Palace Road
Hammersmith
London
W6 8JB

Browse the complete Collins catalogue at
www.collins.co.uk

© HarperCollins *Publishers* Limited 2014

10 9 8 7 6 5 4 3 2 1
ISBN 978-0-00-754752-4

Caroline Bentley-Davies, Gareth Calway, Robert Francis, Mike Gould, Ian Kirby, Christopher Martin and Keith West assert their moral rights to be identified as the authors of this work.

British Library Cataloguing in Publication Data
A Catalogue record for this publication is available from the British Library.

Commissioned by Catherine Martin
Edited in-house by Alicia Higgins
Project managed and edited by Sonya Newland
Proofread by Kelly Davis
Designed by Joerg Hartmannsgruber
Typeset by 320 Media
Cover design by Angela English
Printed and bound by L.E.G.O S.p.A. Italy

With thanks to Jackie Newman and Kim Williams.

Packaged for HarperCollins by
White-Thomson Publishing Ltd.
www.wtpub.co.uk
+44 (0) 843 208 7460

Acknowledgements

The publishers gratefully acknowledge the permissions granted to reproduce copyright material in this book. While every effort has been made to trace and contact copyright holders, where this has not been possible the publishers will be pleased to make the necessary arrangements at the first opportunity.

Oread by H. D. (Hilda Dolittle) from COLLECTED POEMS 1912-1944 copyright © 1914 by Hilda Dolittle, Reprinted by permission of New Directions Publishing Corp and Carcent Press Limited (p 12); Extract from *Martyn Pig* by Kevin Brooks, text © Kevin Brooks 2002 reproduced by permission of The Chicken House (p 16); Extract from *The Power of Five: Raven's Gate* by Anthony Horowitz, © 2005 Anthony Horowitz, reproduced by permission of Walker Books Ltd, London SE11 5HJ (pp 22, 23); From www.telegraph.co.uk/travel/destination/uk/england/66544/Brighton-city-break-guide.html by Louise Roddon, *The Daily Telegraph*. Reprinted with permission of Telegraph Media Group (p 28); campaign leaflet reprinted by kind permission of AnimalAid (p 36); Change4Life website © Crown Copyright (p 38); extract from *Tribes* by Catherine MacPhail, published by Puffin Books, part of The Penguin Group (p 40); Extracts from *Thursday's Child* by Sonya Hartnett, © 2000 Sonya Hartnett, Published by arrangement with Penguin Books Australia Ltd, and reproduced by permission of Walker Books Ltd, London SE11 5HJ (pp 46, 47); 'Seascape' by Alison Chisholm first published in 'The Need for Unicorns' Stride Publications © Alison Chisholm. Reprinted with kind permission of the author (p 54); Extract from *A Handful of Dust* by Evelyn Waugh, reproduced by permission of The Penguin Group (p 92).

The publishers would like to thank the following for permission to reproduce pictures in these pages:

Cover image and p1 Mikhail Hoboton Popov/Shutterstock

p 5 Botond Horvath/Shutterstock, p 6 Pictorial Press Ltd/Alamy, p 7 © Eoin Coveney/NB Illustration, p 8 Private Collection/Peter Newark American Pictures/The Bridgeman Art Library, p 9 Getty Images, p 10 ronfromyork/Shutterstock, p 11 daseaford/Shutterstock, p 12 Getty Images, p 13 LittleMiss/Shutterstock, p 15 Gail Johnson/Shutterstock, p 16 Vladimir Wrangel/Shutterstock, p. 17 Dasha Petrenko/Shutterstock, p 19 Watchtheworld/Shutterstock, p 20 FilmMagic/Getty Images, p 21 Getty Images, p 22 sint/Shutterstock, p 23 Jochen Schoenfeld/Shutterstock, p 24 ketmanee sriput/Shutterstock, p 25 maximult/Shutterstock, p 26 Paul Thomas/Stringer/Getty Images, p 28 Lance Bellers/Shutterstock, p 29 Gail Johnson/Shutterstock, p 31 Lidante/Shutterstock, p 32 Calvin & Hobbes cartoon © 1993 Watterson. Reprinted by permission of UNIVERSAL UCLICK. All rights reserved, p 33 Lewis Tse Pui Lung/Shutterstock, p 34 Natalia Bratslavsky/Shutterstock, p 35 Eak/Shutterstock, p 39 Andrei Zarubaika/Shutterstock, p 40 Richard Peterson/Shutterstock, p 42 Alexander Hohenlohe Burr/Getty Images, p 45 Samot/Shutterstock, p 46 Getty Images, p 47 Natali Zakharova/Shutterstock, p 48 Image Asset Management Ltd./Alamy, p 50 auremar/Shutterstock, p 51 Kuzma/Shutterstock, p 52 Pavel L Photo and Video/Shutterstock, p 53 Marcin Balcerzak/Shutterstock, p 54 olgashevtsova/Shutterstock, p 57 Lisa S./Shutterstock, p 58 Lebrecht Music and Arts Photo Library/Alamy, p 59 Ssokolov/Shutterstock, p 60 Getty Images, p 62 Moviestore collection Ltd/Alamy, p 63 Anneka/Shutterstock, p 65 Getty Images, p 66 Alex Hubenov/Shutterstock, p 68 Lisa S./Shutterstock, p 69 Ben Jeayes/Shutterstock, p 71 Diana Halstead/Shutterstock, p 73 Mary Evans Picture Library/Alamy, p 74 360b/Shutterstock, p 75 Rafal Olechowski/Shutterstock, p 76 Alan Poulson Photography/Shutterstock, p 77 Adam Tinney/Shutterstock, p 78 Classic Image/Alamy, p 79 Getty Images, p 80 MarkMirror/Shutterstock, p 82 Peter Alvey/Alamy, p 85 alphaspirit/Shutterstock, p 87 Somchai Som/Shutterstock, p 89 Dominik Hladik/Shutterstock, p 90 BestPhotoStudio/Shutterstock, p 92 Steve Silver Smith/Shutterstock, p 95 Wutthichai/Shutterstock, p 96 danilo ducak/Shutterstock, p 98 CandyBox Images/Shutterstock, p 100 Rich Koele/Shutterstock, p 101 Goran Bogicevic/Shutterstock.

Contents

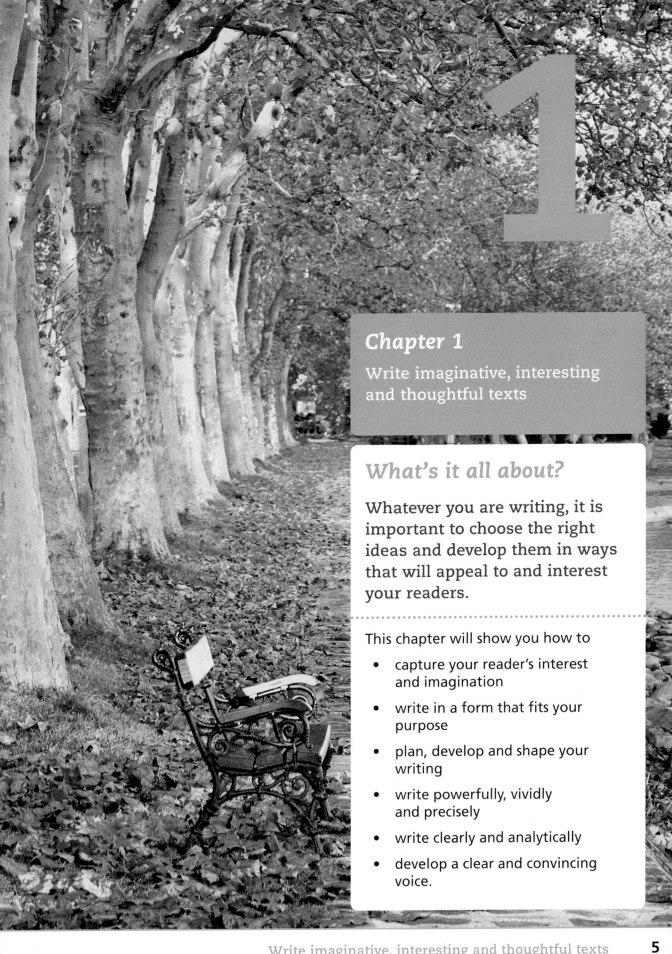

1

Chapter 1

Write imaginative, interesting and thoughtful texts

What's it all about?

Whatever you are writing, it is important to choose the right ideas and develop them in ways that will appeal to and interest your readers.

This chapter will show you how to

- capture your reader's interest and imagination
- write in a form that fits your purpose
- plan, develop and shape your writing
- write powerfully, vividly and precisely
- write clearly and analytically
- develop a clear and convincing voice.

Capture your reader's interest and imagination

Learning objective

- bring your writing to life with imaginative detail.

The poet John Keats said that when he watched a sparrow, he felt himself 'pick about the gravel' with the bird. In order to *write* well, you need to *imagine* well.

Getting you thinking

What would it be like to be violently kidnapped and never see your home again? Read this account in the personal voice of Olaudah Equiano, an **Igbo** boy born in 1745 who was kidnapped and enslaved at the age of 11. Here, after months travelling as a prisoner, he reaches the sea.

Olaudah Equiano

> The first object which **saluted** my eyes when I arrived on the coast was the sea, and a slave ship. These filled me with astonishment, which was soon **converted** to terror. When I was carried on board, I was immediately handled, and tossed up to see if I were sound by some of the crew; and I was now persuaded that I had gotten into a world of bad spirits, and that they were going to kill me. When I looked round the ship too, and saw a large furnace of copper boiling, and a multitude of black people chained together, every one of their **countenances** expressing **dejection** and sorrow, I no longer doubted of my fate, and, quite overpowered with horror and **anguish**, I fell motionless on the deck and fainted.
>
> *The Interesting Narrative* by Olaudah Equiano

Glossary

Igbo: group of people from the area that is now south-east Nigeria

saluted: met

converted: turned

countenances: faces

dejection: sadness or hopelessness

anguish: worry

1 With a partner, pick out five details that help you to imagine Olaudah's suffering.

Now join with another pair to compare and discuss your choices.

How does it work?

Olaudah describes what he could see so that his reader can experience it. He shares his feelings (the nouns: 'terror', 'horror', 'anguish') and expresses *how it seemed to him at the time* ('I had gotten into a world of bad spirits'). He also uses strong verbs ('overpowered', 'handled', 'tossed', 'chained').

Now you try it

2 Imagine you have been kidnapped and taken prisoner on this slave ship. In your own *voice*, make notes on your experiences as you are taken on board and the ship sets sail into the unknown. Think about

a) what you can see (*the chains, the rats, other slaves*)

b) what you can hear (*the sailors yelling at you in a language you don't understand*)

c) what you can smell (*the suffocating smells of people cramped together*)

d) what your thoughts and feelings are (*fear, terror, misery?*).

> **Top tip**
>
> Try to find strong nouns and powerful verbs that create a vivid picture of the scene. Describe the experience in a way that your reader can 'see' or sense.

Apply your skills

3 Look at the picture of a slave ship below.

a) What do you think conditions were like for prisoners on these ships? Add these new details to your notes.

b) Turn your notes into a set of diary entries describing your experiences on the ship. Write them in a way that makes your reader *see*, *hear* and *smell* the atmosphere on board.

Check your progress

Some progress »
I can use some imaginative detail in my writing.

Good progress »»
I can use the senses to capture my reader's imagination.

Excellent progress »»»
I can choose strong words to write and imagine in convincing detail.

Write in a form that fits your purpose

Choosing the right type of text means thinking about *why* you are writing and *who for*. You need to choose the right form for your *audience* and *purpose*.

Getting you thinking

Read this extract from an 18th-century anti-slavery poem.

The Sorrows of Yamba

Then for love of filthy Gold,
　　Strait they bore me to the sea;
Cramm'd me down a Slave Ship's hold,
　　Where were Hundreds stow'd like me [...]

At the savage Captain's beck,
　　Now like Brutes they make us prance;
Smack the **Cat** about the Deck,
　　And in scorn they bid us dance.

Nauseous horse beans they bring nigh,
　　Sick and sad we cannot eat;
Cat must cure the Sulks they cry,
　　Down their throats we'll force the **meat** [...]

Driven like Cattle to a fair,
　　See they sell us young and old;
Child from Mother too they tear
　　All for love of filthy Gold .

Hannah More

1 How does the poet get across her message about slavery? Find examples of

- **a)** repeated words or phrases

- **b)** contrasts (for example, 'us' and 'them')

- **c)** words that suggest cruelty (for example, 'savage').

2 With a partner, talk about what form you could use to get across an anti-slavery message today. Which do you think would be most effective:

- **a)** a letter to a newspaper

- **b)** a Facebook post

- **c)** a leaflet to support a campaign

Glossary

Cat: a kind of whip

Nauseous: sickening

meat: any form of food

d) a rap song

e) a website

f) a persuasive speech to Parliament?

How does it work?

The poem gets across its message effectively – the evidence of suffering is strong but the emotion is controlled. It narrates shocking facts that were 'news' to the reader of that time, like a newspaper story. The rhymes and rhythms make it catchy to chant or sing. All of this makes it ideal as a 'campaign' text.

When choosing the right form for a modern anti-slavery text, you need to think about

- who you want to convince

- who you want to join your campaign

- whether you need to be formal or informal to persuade them.

Now you try it

If you were describing the events of the poem in a speech in court at the trial of one of the ship's crew, you would need to use more **formal language**.

3 Imagine a judge instructs the narrator, Yamba:

'Give this court an account of your treatment aboard the slave ship.'

Put yourself in Yamba's place and give account of the journey. Use details from the poem, but keep your tone factual and let the facts speak for themselves.

Apply your skills

4 Step into role as a journalist. Write a report of an interview with Yamba, describing her experiences. Use details from the poem in your report, but remember to put her words into the **third person** or into quotation marks.

Choose a striking headline for your piece (for example, 'Slave's terrible ordeal').

Glossary

formal language: language that uses standard, professional-sounding words and phrases

third person: a point of view that uses 'he', 'she' or 'it' when referring to a person or idea, rather than 'I' or 'you'

Check your progress

Some progress

I can select and report some details from the poem.

Good progress

I can write a short article in the third person.

Excellent progress

I can choose details from the poem and shape them into an appropriate form for my report.

Plan, develop and shape your writing

Learning objective
- write from a plan.

You should always plan your writing in a way that helps you to record the right ideas and organise them in the most effective way to suit your purpose.

Getting you thinking

Imagine you are a police officer who has been called to the scene of a car crash. When you arrive, this is what you see:

- The accident seems to have involved a head-on collision between a police car – which is now on fire – and a car full of joyriders.
- Both police officers are injured, one badly, and the driver of the other car seems to have a serious head injury.
- A female joyrider in the passenger seat is screaming and has blood gushing from her leg, whilst in the back seat another male passenger seems uninjured but is just sitting there in shock.
- You also see a teenage boy who appears to be running away from the scene.

1 With a partner, role-play a conversation over the police radio between the police officer on the scene and the radio operator at the police station. Think about what key information needs to be given and in what order. What questions would the radio operator ask?

2 You will have to write an official report of the incident later, but you need to plan it first. Which of these formats would be the most useful for planning a report:
- a flow chart
- a spider diagram
- a table or chart
- a bullet-point list or numbered list?

How does it work?

In the role-play, you might have given the life-or-death information about the accident first (requesting a fire engine to deal with the blaze) or about the most seriously injured people (asking for an ambulance).

However, in planning your report, a *flow chart* or *list* would help you to organise the information about the incident in the order in which it occurred.

Now you try it

3 Plan your official report. Think about what information you should give. You could include

a) a description of where the accident took place

b) statements from witnesses, the joyriders and police officers involved in the accident

c) any other details you noticed when you arrived on the scene.

Consider what *order* all this information needs to be presented in.

Apply your skills

A superior officer tells you:

> Report writing is *factual* writing; keep it formal – logical, concise and official. This is not the time to show off your poetic talent, storytelling or descriptive skills!

4 Keeping her advice in mind, write your report. Base it on the plan you have made and include all the details you noted from the scene of the accident.

5 Add a closing statement about which driver you believe caused the accident. Remember that your opinion must come at the *end* of the report – after you have described the facts of the case.

Check your progress

Some progress
I can create a simple plan for my report.

Good progress
I can write a clear factual report from my plan.

Excellent progress
I can organise, plan and write a concise report with a clear closing statement.

Write powerfully, vividly and precisely

Learning objectives

- express strong feelings in sharp images
- use imagery in your writing.

The best imaginative writing uses vivid imagery to create pictures in the reader's mind, but is also precise, keeping details in sharp focus.

Getting you thinking

Have you ever wished you could just draw what you mean, instead of having to find the right words?

1 Make quick pencil sketches of what you mean by these words:

a) loudmouth

b) bighead.

2 Now read these two poems and draw the images they create in your mind.

A Touch of Cold in the Autumn Night

A touch of cold in the autumn night –
I walked **abroad**
And saw the **ruddy** moon lean over a hedge
Like a red-faced farmer.

T. E. Hulme

Oread

Whirl up, sea –
whirl your pointed pines,
splash your great pines
on our rocks,
hurl your green over us,
cover us with your pools of fir.

H.D.

---

3 Compare your drawings with a partner's. Do you think 'Oread' is a description of the sea compared to a forest, or a forest compared to the sea?

Glossary

abroad: outside in the open

ruddy: red or pink

How does it work?

Both extracts use effective imagery – including similes and metaphors – to conjure up pictures in the reader's mind. The writers have made precise and deliberate word choices in order to achieve this.

Think of someone who you have very powerful feelings about – positive or negative. It can't be anyone in the room and you must keep the person's identity secret.

4 Now imagine them as a piece of furniture. Would they be

a) a battered but very comfortable old armchair

b) a sleek leather sofa with an adjustable footrest

c) a hard plastic stool?

5 With a partner, take it in turns to describe the person you have chosen by answering these questions:

a) What type of movement would this person be? (the curl of the wind on the surface of a wave...)

b) What season would this person be? (a cold windy autumn with damp and dying leaves crackling underfoot...)

c) What time of day would this person be? (the moment when you just want to go home between last lesson and detention!)

Apply your skills

6 Write a poem of seven or eight lines about the person you have described. Use the best images you have come up with.

Think about how you could develop your imaginative word choices. If you said this person would be 'winter', extend the metaphor by describing exactly what kind of winter they are:

You are...

A cruel, frosty winter biting my toes...

When you have written a first draft, review and revise your poem by

- cutting any unnecessary filler words or phrases

- changing the order of lines to focus the reader's attention

- dropping any weaker lines that don't add to the image.

> **Top tip**
>
> A *simile* says that something is *like* something else. A *metaphor* just says that something *is* something else. Look back at the poems and try to find examples of both.

Check your progress

Some progress
I can include some of my images in a poem.

Good progress
I can choose and develop imaginative images in a poem.

Excellent progress
I can create and sequence striking images in a poem.

Write clearly and analytically

Learning objective
- analyse a subject and write about it in a measured way.

When analysing texts, it is important to use facts and figures and to weigh up different possibilities. You must also pick the right sort of language and **tone** for your purpose.

Glossary

tone: the way something sounds

Getting you thinking

1 In pairs, read aloud the statements below about the effects of tourism on rural England.

   a) Do they agree with each other?

   b) How would you describe the tone of each?

> I've got to change schools now because Dad's work has moved to King's Lynn. I reckon it's all these tourists coming here. There's an invasion of 'Chelsea tractors' taking over our town!

> It could be argued that tourists are damaging English rural life. Locals are unable to afford the high prices Londoners pay to use the cottages as second homes.

How does it work?

A similar viewpoint is expressed in different tones.

The first speaker *sounds* biased ('I reckon it's all these tourists...') and her joke about 'Chelsea tractors' (SUVs) isn't appropriate in a formal, analytical piece.

The second speaker *analyses* the problem. The tone is reasonable ('it could be argued') and it uses clear facts.

Top tip

Analysis typically uses formal language, reasons and facts. Writing that expresses an opinion often uses informal, direct and simple sentences and emotion.

Now you try it

2 Study the following facts about rural England. What do they suggest about the importance of tourism?

Only 2% of Norfolk people work in farming. 9% of Norfolk people work in the tourist industry. That is comparable with Brighton (10.7%), Devon (10.6%) and Dorset (10.1%), if not quite with Cornwall and the Scilly Isles (14.9%) and the biggest UK tourist centre of all, the resort of Torbay (16.7%).

Figures from the Office of National Statistics

3 On holiday in Norfolk, you meet a farmer who is angry about tourists walking across, picnicking and pitching tents in their fields. Act out a conversation, quoting the facts and statistics above. Start

> Oi! That field's not for holidaymakers – it's my workplace!

> Sorry, we got lost! But actually, nine per cent…

4 Look at this speech.

> You might agree with our mum, the village post-mistress. She says holidaymakers buy up all the cottages here, but they drive into town instead of using local shops. As a result, she has no customers.

a) What language features (for example, formal words or phrases) create a *reasoned* tone?

b) What language sounds *biased*?

5 Now turn this speech into a paragraph of *analysis*. Begin:

> It might be argued that tourism has delivered more problems than benefits. For instance, while it is true that…

Remember to use facts, examples and language that sounds reasonable.

Apply your skills

6 What do *you* think are the pros and cons of tourism in country areas? Write up your thoughts, weighing up both sides. State your views in a *reasoned* way.

Check your progress

Some progress

I can use some facts and figures in my writing.

Good progress

I can give my opinion clearly and make some reference to an opposing view.

Excellent progress

I can write clearly and analytically, stating a balanced view in a measured tone.

Develop a clear and convincing voice

Learning objective

- choose and develop a narrative voice.

When you are writing fiction, you create a 'voice' that is telling the story. This is particularly true when you are telling a story in the first person (using 'I').

Getting you thinking

Read this extract from a novel called *Martyn Pig.* Martyn is telling the story.

> I wasn't that worried when she didn't show up the following morning. Not at first anyway. Annoyed, maybe. But not worried. Alex was often late. She could never understand why it bothered me. 'I'm here now, aren't I?' she'd say. She was right, in a way. If you like someone enough, it doesn't matter how long they keep you waiting – as long as they turn up in the end, it's all right. I can't help it, though. I hate waiting for someone to turn up. I can't understand why anyone should be late for anything. Unless something disastrous happens there's no reason for it. No reason at all. I'm never late for anything.
>
> *Martyn Pig* by Kevin Brooks

1 What impression do you get of Martyn?

   a) What do you find out about his thoughts and feelings? For example, is he anxious or relaxed?

   b) What words or phrases give you this impression?

2 Is Martyn's 'voice' *informal* (chatty and friendly) or is it quite *formal*? Does he ramble or is he precise?

How does it work?

Writing in the *first person* means you only tell the story from one point of view – that of the *narrator*, who is the main character. As readers, we share this person's thoughts and feelings, and see everything through their eyes.

Careful word choice and sentence construction help create a realistic *voice* for your narrator. The way a person speaks or shares their thoughts can tell the reader a lot.

Here Martyn comes across as an anxious and perhaps pedantic person, as he constantly corrects himself and rephrases statements.

Now you try it

You are going to plan and write a passage in the first person. You are going to be writing from the viewpoint of Alex, the girl Martyn was waiting for.

3 Plan your passage first. Think about these points:

- How can you create the right voice for your narrator?

- What sort of language would she use? Chatty or formal?

- What kind of things would she describe?

- Is she emotional and inward-looking like Martyn, or is she more carefree?

- How do you want the reader to feel about your narrator? Should they like her, trust her, fear her?

- What has happened to her? Why didn't she show up? What does she think of Martyn?

Then write your plan in the form of a bullet-point or numbered list. Outline what you are going to write, in the style and order you will write it.

4 Now draft the opening paragraph from Alex's point of view. Remember to use the first person 'i'.

Apply your skills

5 Draft the rest of your story opening. Try to keep the first person narrative going and describe only what Alex can see or know. Give her a convincing and consistent voice.

Check your progress

Some progress

I can draft an opening paragraph.

Good progress

I can write an opening paragraph using the first person consistently.

Excellent progress

I can sustain a convincing and consistent voice throughout my story opening.

Check your progress

Some progress

- [ ] I can bring my writing to life.
- [ ] I can sometimes choose the best form for my writing.
- [ ] I can create a simple plan for my writing.
- [ ] I can grab the reader's attention.
- [ ] I can recognise formal and biased language.
- [ ] I can create a voice that sometimes rings true.

Good progress

- [ ] I can write imaginatively and thoughtfully.
- [ ] I can select and shape the most appropriate form for my writing.
- [ ] I can organise and plan my writing for my purpose.
- [ ] I can use images to write vividly, powerfully and memorably.
- [ ] I can analyse a subject.
- [ ] I can develop a convincing viewpoint or role.

Excellent progress

- [ ] I can write imaginatively with confidence and purpose.
- [ ] I can develop features of a form for a range of purposes and audiences.
- [ ] I can plan and write in a suitable tone and form.
- [ ] I can write engaging and fluent texts using suitable images.
- [ ] I can analyse a subject and write about it in a balanced way.
- [ ] I can achieve a language (word choice, style, voice, viewpoint) that suits speaker, character or purpose.

Chapter 2

Produce texts that are appropriate to task, reader and purpose

What's it all about?

You need to make sure that the purpose of your writing is clear throughout the texts you write. To achieve this, you must choose the right techniques and level of formality.

This chapter will show you how to

- choose the right tone for persuasive texts

- improve characterisation in narrative and descriptive writing

- use factual information effectively when writing to argue

- use the active and passive for different effects in non-fiction writing

- write in an appropriate style for your purpose.

Choose the right tone for persuasive texts

Learning objective

- use different techniques to get formality and purpose right.

You need to choose the right level of *formality* for your audience and think about the different *writing techniques* you can use to achieve your purpose.

Getting you thinking

Imagine you have been asked to persuade a celebrity to visit your school to raise money for a new drama room.

Read the opening paragraphs from one student's letter to Benedict Cumberbatch, the star of *Sherlock*.

Dear Benedict,

I have often thought of writing to Sherlock Holmes to help me solve my maths homework, only to realise he is not real! This is how convincing your acting is, but I am aware that it takes a lot of hard work and skill to act so well. School is often the place where students first experience drama; perhaps you remember your days at school when you first started acting? If so, then you will know that having a proper space to develop your skills is vital.

The problem we want you to solve is this: how can we turn an old gym into a state-of-the art, soundproofed drama studio? In fact, we think we know the answer – but we still need your help.

Our school is running a fund-raising talent show on 24th November and it would be wonderful if you could offer just a few hours of your valuable time to present the awards to the winners. Just imagine how many more tickets we would sell if people knew Sherlock was attending! Wouldn't it be great, too, to know that your invaluable support had meant pupils in the school can all have a chance of becoming television stars?

1 Who is the *audience* for this letter, and what is the writer's *purpose*?

2 Has he or she got the *tone* right, or is it too chatty or too serious? What words or phrases make you think this?

The writer uses a *formal style*:

- The letter is polite but friendly, complimenting Benedict on his work and using formal words and phrases ('I am aware', 'develop your skills').

- The writer uses complete sentences, rather than short, abbreviated sentences, and full words rather than contractions ('I have' not 'I've').

The writer also uses *persuasive language*:

- *Positive adjectives* show what the outcome of Benedict's involvement will be ('state-of-the-art, soundproofed') and are used to flatter him ('your *invaluable* support').

- **Rhetorical questions** make Benedict think about the effect of his help.

Glossary

Rhetorical questions: questions that don't need an answer

Now you try it

Now read the opening of a similar letter to Mo Farah.

> Hiya Mo!!!
>
> I am Ben in Year 9 and I am in charge of our tutor group's charity fund-raiser at Four Green School. We're raising some cash for a children's charity in Thailand. We're having this fete – you could come. You're famous. Are you mates with Usain Bolt? I'd love to meet him even more than you...

3 Rewrite the opening of the letter to make it more persuasive and suitably formal.

Apply your skills

4 Write a letter to persuade a celebrity to visit your school to raise money for charity. Think about

a) how you will clearly state your purpose

b) what you need to tell them about the event

c) what persuasive techniques you will use

d) how you will make your letter sound formal.

Check your progress

Some progress

I can make the main purpose of my letter clear.

Good progress

I can use some persuasive techniques and write with appropriate formality.

Excellent progress

I can choose the right level of formality and use a range of persuasive techniques.

Improve characterisation in narrative and descriptive writing

Knowing how to build a convincing character in narratives is key to keeping your readers engaged.

Getting you thinking

Read these opening lines in an extract from the novel *Raven's Gate*.

> Matt Freeman knew he was making a mistake.
>
> He was sitting on a low wall outside Ipswich station, wearing a grey hooded sweatshirt, shapeless, faded jeans, and trainers with frayed laces.
>
> *Raven's Gate* by Anthony Horowitz

1 In what ways is this a good introduction to a character? Think about

  a) the questions it raises

  b) how well it creates a picture in your mind.

How does it work?

Writers use many techniques to create interesting characters:

- direct description (adjectives describing how a character looks; verbs and adverbs to describe how he or she moves or acts)

- **metaphors** and **similes** (comparing the character to something else)

- showing or telling you how other people react to the character

- showing or telling you what the character thinks.

Glossary

metaphors: comparisons between two things that aren't literally alike

similes: comparisons between two things using the words 'like' or 'as'

Here is the next part of the extract:

It was six o'clock in the evening and the London train had just pulled in. Behind him, commuters were fighting their way out of the station. The concourse was a tangle of cars, taxis and pedestrians, all of them trying to find their way home. A traffic light blinked from red to green but nothing moved. Somebody leant on their horn and the noise blared out, cutting through the damp evening air. Matt heard it and looked up briefly. But the crowd meant nothing to him. He wasn't part of it. He had never been – and sometimes thought he never would be.

Two men carrying umbrellas walked past and glanced at him disapprovingly. They probably thought he was up to no good. The way he was sitting – hunched forward with his knees apart – made him look somehow dangerous, and older than fourteen. He had broad shoulders, a well developed, muscular body and very bright blue, intelligent eyes. His hair was black, cut very short. Give him another five years he could be a footballer or a model – or, like plenty of others, both.

His first name was Matthew but he had always called himself Matt. As the troubles had begun to pile up in his life, he had used his surname less and less until it was no longer part of him...

2 Which of the techniques listed does the writer use to give you a sense of Matt's character? By the end, what new questions are raised in the reader's mind?

3 Using some of the techniques, write one paragraph about a character called Dina.

   a) In your first sentence, place her in a setting ('Dina stood by...').

   b) In your second sentence, write a short description of her appearance ('She was wearing...').

   c) In your third sentence, tell us one thing about her thoughts or feelings ('Dina felt....').

Check your progress

Apply your skills

In the extract above, the writer begins by describing the scene, then slowly zooms in on Matt's appearance and then tells us his thoughts.

4 Look at the picture on the right. Write two or three paragraphs introducing this character, using the same technique.

Use factual information effectively when writing to argue

Learning objective

- use and organise factual information and language when arguing a point of view.

When arguing a point of view, the language you use and the way you select and organise factual information can help you achieve your purpose.

Getting you thinking

Read this short script of a TV debate:

> **Activist:** People should be banned from keeping exotic pets. Loads of them are set free every day because their owners can't be bothered to look after them. It's disgraceful!

> **Expert:** Clearly, members of the public have a duty to care for non-native species responsibly, but the reality is that there were only 12 cases last month of such pets being released. And 30 per cent of these were accidental. These are definitely not reasons to ban exotic pets altogether.

1. What are the two viewpoints being expressed here?

2. What evidence does each person give to support their view?

3. Which person provides factual **data** to support their view?

Glossary

data: facts and statistics (numbers)

How does it work?

When presenting an argument, *objective* language is the most persuasive. Note how the expert uses

- formal, professional-sounding language ('members of the public')

- adverbs to stress his opinion ('Clearly')

- facts and statistics ('12 cases last month') to back up his argument and sound both precise and convincing.

Top tip

You can use facts selectively to make your point. The expert mentions '12 cases last month' but over a year this would work out at almost 150 – which sounds much more!

Read the article below:

> I reckon anyone would think we hate our furry friends when you see those stories about people dumping their animals, but I'm sure we really love our pets in the UK! Just think of all the households that have at least one pet. Millions, I bet! Dogs and cats are dead popular. There are loads and loads of them, which proves how much we love them! Then there's fish – crikey, there must be loads more of them than dogs and cats! Just think of the ones indoors and outdoors. Pets make us happy too – think of all the joy they bring. We love pets!!

4 Look at the statistics below. Now rewrite the article using some or all of the facts to support the argument that Britain is a nation of pet lovers.

Use a more formal and less personal tone.

Pet facts

- 13 million households (48%) in UK have at least one pet
- Dog and cat population: approx. 8 million each
- 23% of UK households have at least one dog
- 19% of UK households have at least one cat
- Indoor fish: 20–25 million kept in tanks
- Outdoor fish: 20–25 million kept in ponds
- 60% of people with pets say the pet makes them a happier person.

Apply your skills

5 Write the same article, but from the opposing viewpoint. Try to use the same facts, but show that there are lots of people in the UK who *don't* love pets. Remember, your tone should still be formal.

Check your progress

Some progress
I can present a straightforward viewpoint in my writing.

Good progress
I can use facts to develop a clear viewpoint in my writing.

Excellent progress
I can use factual information creatively but in a formal tone when arguing a case.

Use the active and passive for different effects in non-fiction writing

Active and passive voices are useful when you want to draw attention to particular ideas, facts or people.

Getting you thinking

Read these two short headlines:

> # Jess wins 100 metres in record time

> # 100 metres won in record time

1 Which headline do you think comes from a local newspaper and which from a sports website read by people around the world? How do you know?

How does it work?

The *active voice* can be used to show clearly – or draw attention to – the *subject* of the sentence (doing the action). For example:

Usain Bolt breaks world record!

— subject

— verb

The *passive voice* is used when the subject is moved or removed:

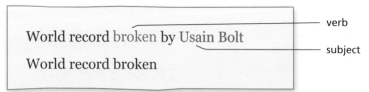

World record broken by Usain Bolt

World record broken

— verb

— subject

The passive draws attention to what has been or is being done, rather than the person/doer – for example, if the fact of the world record being broken is more important than who broke it.

Read the first part of this memo from a games teacher to his head teacher.

> Re: Why sports day was cancelled
>
> Chairs had been put out, and parents welcomed, when it was noticed that the weather was deteriorating. Shelter was offered in the old pavilion but unfortunately the rain became worse, and by 2.30pm there was no option but to abandon the event.

2 List at least three examples of phrases or sentences in the *passive voice*. Why did the teacher use the passive voice to explain the cancellation?

3 Here is the final part of the memo. Rewrite it, changing the passive forms to active ones ('I can send...'). What is the effect of your changes?

> A letter of apology can be sent out to parents and a new date for sports day can be provided.

Apply your skills

4 Below are some notes by a war reporter about a city under siege. Write a full version of the report so the focus is on *the city* not the attackers.

Include an appropriate headline and add any further details you wish.

> Rebel army and its occupation of city
>
> 5pm local time: rebel army surrounds city
>
> Midnight: rebel soldiers breach defences
>
> Daybreak: I hear cries and shouts for help from the city's inhabitants
>
> Soon after: soldiers release women and children unharmed
>
> Midday: rebels take over radio station – I hear message saying rebels now in total control of city
>
> Rebels raise flag and fire guns to celebrate victory

Top tip

Including a few active forms will add some drama to your report.

Check your progress

Some progress

I can recognise the difference between the active and passive voices in texts.

Good progress

I can write my report using mostly the passive voice.

Excellent progress

I can move between the passive and active voices to create a dramatic report.

Write in an appropriate style for your purpose

Learning objective

- change the style of your writing to suit your purpose.

Texts can be about the same topic, but their purposes can be quite different. You need to adapt your writing technique to suit your purpose.

Getting you thinking

Here are two texts about Brighton:

> Brighton is a seaside resort with a pier and a pleasure beach. There are over 21,000 students living in Brighton. There are many shops, cafés and places of interest in Brighton, including the Royal Pavilion. Each May, the city hosts the Brighton and Fringe festivals, the second largest Arts Festival in Britain.

> You need never get bored in this lovably eccentric city. There's always something unexpected to enjoy – be it a sea-facing yoga class, watching a skateboarding Jack Russell, or browsing through a surprisingly good beachfront hippy market. The secret is to roam freely and keep your eyes peeled [...]
>
> Head to the **boho** North Laine, and you find offbeat designers and dingy flea markets happily melding with sleek restaurants and bars. Throw in **gentrified** Regency squares, oddball museums, and a clutch of well upholstered parks with traditional cafés attached – and you have a city that truly caters for all tastes.
>
> Louise Roddon, *The Daily Telegraph*

1 What is the *purpose* of each text? Think about

a) who the audience might be

b) the way the writer addresses the reader (for example, the use of imperative verbs in the second text)

c) the descriptions of particular places (which one uses more vivid adjectives?)

Glossary

boho: unconventional and arty

gentrified: when a building has been restored or upgraded

Read this factual description of the Isle of Anglesey:

> Anglesey is separated from the mainland of north-west Wales by the Menai Strait in the Irish Sea. There are cliffs, beaches and mountains. Anglesey has one of the driest climates in Wales. There are two RSPB parks. There are 15,000 visitors every summer. Most of the coastline has been designated an Area of Outstanding Beauty. Seals, dolphins and whales have been seen in the coastal waters.

2 Turn this into a persuasive text. Use some of the techniques used in the *Telegraph* article:

- imperative verbs to 'make' people want to visit
- vivid and positive adjectives ('*spectacular* cliffs')
- referring to the reader directly ('you')
- giving a specific detail of a typical sight or person doing something that sticks in the memory.

Apply your skills

Here are some notes made by a journalist about an enjoyable winter visit to Brighton.

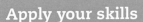

My December day trip

Was much quieter, but not dead like other seaside resorts.

Good big shops for Christmas shopping, as well as small vintage ones hidden away.

Still lots to see and do: cafés, clubs and bars, the pier.

Nice walk on promenade – big waves, dark clouds – atmospheric.

Hot chocolate in a beachfront cafe, watched sunset over sea.

Train back to London at 6pm – sorry to say goodbye.

3 Write this up as a full account, providing detail and a vivid picture of the town at this time of year. Remember – this is a narrative account, so it will read and be structured more like a story but it will still give a positive picture.

Check your progress
....

Some progress
I can adapt some of the information I am given to create another text.

Good progress
I can use the information I am given and different techniques to match a certain purpose.

Excellent progress
I can confidently adapt information and techniques to create different types of writing.

Check your progress

Some progress

- I can make my main purpose clear.
- I can use some descriptive details to bring a character to life.
- I can present a straightforward viewpoint in my writing.
- I can recognise the difference between the active and passive voice in texts.
- I can adapt some of the information I am given to create another text.

Good progress

- I can use some persuasive techniques and write with appropriate formality.
- I can use both descriptive vocabulary and other techniques to create character.
- I can use facts to develop a clear viewpoint in my writing.
- I can write a report using mostly the passive voice.
- I can use the information I am given and different techniques to match a certain purpose.

Excellent progress

- I can choose the right level of formality and use a range of persuasive techniques.
- I can use a range of writing techniques to create an interesting character.
- I can use factual information creatively but in a formal tone when arguing a case.
- I can move between the passive and active voice to create a dramatic report.
- I can confidently adapt information and techniques to create different types of writing.

3

Chapter 3
Organise and present whole texts effectively, sequencing and structuring information, ideas and events

What's it all about?

You need to organise and present texts in ways that fit your purpose for writing and appeal to your target readers. The structure of the text should make your purpose clear and hold your reader's attention.

This chapter will show you how to

- structure your writing clearly
- build your ideas across a piece of writing
- organise and present a text for audience and purpose
- summarise and adapt information clearly
- organise narrative writing effectively
- make your ending link back to your opening.

Structure your writing clearly

Learning objective

• structure your writing well.

A clear structure helps your reader understand what you are trying to say and where your writing is going. The way you structure your writing will depend on the purpose of the text.

Getting you thinking

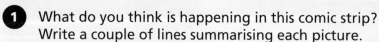

1 What do you think is happening in this comic strip? Write a couple of lines summarising each picture.

How does it work?

The writer of this comic strip put the events into an order the reader can easily follow. It's a simple **chronological** narrative – in time order (for example, there are no flashbacks). There are two *viewpoints*. We go from Calvin's point of view to other people's and then back.

Glossary

chronological: arranged in the order in which things happened

Different structures are more appropriate for different kinds of texts:

- When you are writing to *explain*, you may choose to explore different aspects of your topic in turn, point by point.

- When you are writing to *argue*, you may choose to give one point of view first and then a contrasting point of view. You might then offer your own conclusion.

Now you try it

Waiting for someone to arrive at a station is incredibly annoying. You're bored because you can't go anywhere. You are also anxious – will they turn up?

2 Imagine the person never turns up at all. Write down three other feelings you have when you realise that he or she isn't coming.

3 Now imagine you want to send an email to that person telling him or her how upset you felt. The *purpose* of your email is to explain your feelings – not to tell a story.

Give each point its own sentence. You could start with the most powerful feeling:

I was incredibly upset when you didn't turn up at the station today…

In addition, I felt…

4 In pairs, list six excuses that the person who didn't turn up might give. Be as realistic as possible. ('I was attacked by a Martian' is not a convincing excuse!)

Write each excuse as a sentence.

Apply your skills

Look at the Calvin and Hobbes cartoon again. Remember, it shows two viewpoints – one person waiting, one arriving.

5 In pairs, plan your own comic-book account of waiting at the station for someone who is late. Plan and sketch visuals of the delays and of the excuses given.

Your comic strip should be *chronological* but show *two viewpoints*.

Top tip

You probably experienced the most powerful feeling towards the end of your wait, but because you are writing to *explain*, you don't need to describe things in the order in which they took place.

Check your progress

Some progress

I can organise ideas in a logical sequence.

Good progress

I can organise my ideas logically with some consideration of purpose.

Excellent progress

I can order and sequence my ideas well to help my reader understand the overall direction of my writing.

Build your ideas across a piece of writing

Learning objective

- link ideas across several paragraphs.

When you are writing, you need to stay focused on your topic and keep your ideas connected throughout.

Getting you thinking

Read this extract about a trip to Death Valley, California.

The next morning I awoke ready to see exactly how evil this unforgiving part of the globe could be. My room was cool enough with the air conditioning working full-time to cope with the heat's force. As I stepped out onto the porch in front of my room, it was as if someone had clapped their hand on my shoulder and said 'No you don't!' I took a deep breath as I headed forward, wading through the heat's powerful waves to the **sanctuary** of the breakfast room. It was still only 8 o'clock!

An hour later, full of waffles and maple syrup, I headed outside once more. It was difficult to breathe as I **trudged** back through the burning heat to pack my things for the next leg of our journey. I felt like a deep-sea diver who had run out of air and was desperately trying to get to the surface…

I stopped further into the Valley and realised why it was so aptly named Death Valley. The **stifling** heat seemed to surge into the car as I opened the door, foolishly trying to plunge into its **volcanic domain**. I forced my way forward, my feet sticking to the tarmac on the road as everything, including me, seemed to melt. This was no place for people, or any living thing, and yet there was a group of tourists trying to inch their way towards the summit of what seemed like Everest.

Glossary

sanctuary: a place offering protection

trudged: walked wearily

stifling: suffocating

volcanic domain: like being inside a volcano

1. What theme (or subject) is built throughout this piece of writing?

2. Why does the writer start new paragraphs where he does?

3. How does he link each paragraph with the next one?

How does it work?

The extract is about Death Valley and its intense heat. The writer compares being there to extreme experiences such as deep-sea diving and climbing Everest. He uses powerful adjectives to describe the heat ('evil', 'unforgiving', 'volcanic').

The writer also uses connecting words and phrases ('and', 'yet') and adverbials ('An hour later'). These descriptions and comparisons reveal a common theme and help to link and build ideas throughout the piece.

Now you try it

4. Plan a short account of some extreme weather conditions you have experienced. It could be a very hot day by the sea or just an intensely cold wait at a bus stop! Plan three paragraphs. Think about the following:

   - What *order* will you put the information in?

   - What *connecting words* will you use to link sentences and paragraphs?

   - What *nouns*, *adjectives*, *verbs* and *adverbs* could you use to describe your surroundings?

   - What *similes* or *metaphors* will help build up the intensity of the experience?

Apply your skills

5. Now write your account based on your plan. Structure your writing carefully. Make sure you link and develop ideas across your three paragraphs, keeping the focus on the main theme.

Check your progress

Some progress

I can organise my ideas simply, using linking words and phrases.

Good progress

I can develop my ideas effectively across three paragraphs of description.

Excellent progress

I can structure and sequence my ideas carefully to create a cohesive and interesting description.

Organise and present a text for audience and purpose

Learning objective

- use sentences, paragraphs and presentational devices for effect.

It is important to present your work clearly and effectively so that a reader can easily understand what you have to say. Using different presentational techniques and devices can encourage your audience to read on. They can also reveal exactly what the text is and who it is aimed at.

Getting you thinking

Look at this leaflet from an Animal Aid campaign.

1. In groups of four, make a list of all the *presentational devices* the leaflet designer has used.

2 What is the main message of the leaflet? Who do you think it is aimed at?

How does it work?

Many devices can be used to attract the reader's interest and help the writer achieve his or her purpose. These include

- *pictures* to get across a message or attract attention

- *headings and sub-headings* to signal what the piece is about and to help the reader find information quickly

- *paragraphs, bullet points or numbers* to break up and order information

- *font (style and size)* to show the reader which text is more important and should be read first

- *colour* – for example, the pale greens and browns in the leaflet here create a dull and sickly mood, in contrast to the sunny gold of the cover picture

- a *call to action* to focus the reader's attention on the purpose of the piece.

> **Top tip**
>
> A text must always look right for its audience and purpose.

Now you try it

3 In pairs, redraft and redesign a section of the Animal Aid leaflet for teenagers (aged 12–16). Think about the presentational choices you could make:

- What kind of images would appeal to teenagers?

- What size and style of font will you use?

- What sort of language might appeal to your target audience?

- What other features or techniques could you use?

> **Top tip**
>
> Try to use bullet points to list ideas. These help the reader pick out key ideas more easily.

Apply your skills

4 Now design a leaflet for students in your school, providing information on *one* of the following topics:

- how to deal with bullies

- how to keep fit and healthy.

If you can, use a computer to help with the layout of your leaflet. Remember to choose presentational techniques that will help you achieve your purpose in writing and appeal to your target audience.

Check your progress

Some progress

I can use pictures, headings and colour to present my work effectively on the page.

Good progress

I can use a range of presentational features that suit the purpose and audience of my leaflet.

Excellent progress

I can present texts imaginatively to suit my purpose and audience.

Summarise and adapt information clearly

Learning objective

- summarise and present information in a different way.

Knowing how to summarise information can help you pick out the most important bits of information and present them clearly.

Getting you thinking

In pairs, read this web page.

About Change4Life	Eat well	Get going	Choose less booze	Find local activities	Local supporters

▶ Shopping tips
▶ Cooking & meal ideas
▶ Breakfast
▶ Lunches & picnics
▶ Snacks
▶ Sugar swaps
▶ Cut back on fat
▼ 5 A DAY
    5 A DAY, every day
    What counts as 5 A DAY?
    5 A DAY portion sizes
▶ Watch the salt
▶ Healthy eating tips
▶ Be Food Smart

5 A DAY – tips for getting five portions of fruit and veg each day

Fruit and veg are a source of vitamins, minerals and fibre which may help reduce the risk of diseases like heart disease and some cancers. We all know that it's important for us to eat a variety of at least five portions of fruit and veg each day, but how many of us actually manage it?

Luckily, it can be easier than you think to get your 5 A DAY. The great thing is that you don't need to make a big change to your diet or do without the foods you love.

It doesn't have to be expensive!

It doesn't have to be expensive. You can keep the costs down by buying canned fruit and veg, which doesn't go off as quickly. Choose canned fruit in its own juice – it's healthier than fruit in sugary syrup. Or try canned veg in water with no added salt or sugar.

Frozen is even handier, as you can use what you need and put it back in the freezer! And buying fresh fruit and veg when it's in season is usually cheaper too. Local markets can be great places to pick up fresh and tasty produce at really good prices.

Just add a portion of veg here, sprinkle a portion of fruit there – and you'll hit your 5 A DAY before you know it!

Jo

Is
en
the
up
ad

▶ J
- f

1 Note down all the tips for healthy eating that the page contains.

2 Look at the language and presentational features.

   a) What is the tone of the article?

   b) Is it easy to pick out the key facts? Why or why not?

How does it work?

When summarising and adapting a text, you need to identify the most important pieces of information. Then look at features such as

- language and text structure (Are there long sentences or paragraphs? Is any information repeated? Is the language suitable for the audience?)

- presentational devices (Are the pictures apt? Are the headings clear? Do the colours suit the topic?).

Ask yourself: 'How can I present this more *clearly* and *concisely* and so it *appeals to my audience*?'

Now you try it

3 How could you adapt the web page opposite to get across the information more quickly? Think about using

- short, snappy sentences and **imperatives**

- headings and sub-headings to divide the information appropriately

- bullet points or numbered lists to structure the information clearly

- colours, fonts and text size to make it appealing.

Glossary

imperatives: words or phrases that are commands or requests ('Tidy your room.')

Apply your skills

4 Design a web page for teenagers called 'Nothing feels as healthy as fruit and veg'.

Summarise the information from the web page and from any other sources you can find about healthy eating.

Remember to use presentational features that help you deliver the information *clearly*, *concisely* and *in a way that will appeal to teenagers*.

Check your progress

Some progress
I can summarise the information clearly.

Good progress
I can summarise and present relevant information clearly in a web page.

Excellent progress
I can summarise and present relevant information concisely and so it appeals to my target audience.

Organise narrative writing effectively

When creating a piece of narrative writing, such as a short story or a play, you need to think about the *structure* of your plot.

Getting you thinking

Read this extract from a novel called *Tribes*.

> Kevin gasped and stepped back. In front of him was nothing. He was standing on the edge of a gaping chasm, a hole that stretched to nothingness below. At the other side of that chasm, it looked a million miles away, was a minute stretch of floor and a smashed window. And all that connected the floor Kevin was standing on to that other side was a narrow wooden beam.
>
> Kevin looked at Torry. He was smiling, his hands on his hips. He looked at Doc. There was something **malevolent** in his eyes. And then he looked at Salom. He stepped on to the beam like an acrobat. Kevin gasped.
>
> Salom grinned. 'You get to the other side, and you are a fully paid-up member of the Tribe.'
>
> *Tribes* by Catherine MacPhail

1 In pairs, decide what is happening in the story. Do you think this extract comes at the beginning, the middle or the end of the story?

How does it work?

Your plot might have a *five-part structure*:

- a *beginning* to set up the situation, introducing characters and events (*exposition*)

- *rising action* (perhaps establishing a mystery or a problem to be solved through conflict)

- a *climax* (or turning point)

Top tip

It is vital to plan first, to know where your story is going. Use paragraphs to help structure and organise your ideas.

Glossary

malevolent: evil, nasty

- *falling action* (as things work out towards…)
- a *resolution* of the story (*denouement*).

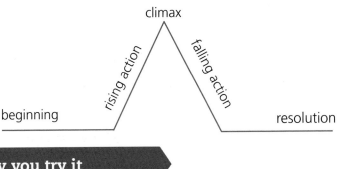

Now you try it

Read the following extracts from the *climax* of two stories.

> That was it! D.I Eames suddenly knew who the killer was. It was Nash's sister all along. She had altered the will and Nash had found out.
>
> Eames picked up his phone. 'Send her in,' he said, grimly…

> The gunmen were closing in. Martin bit his lip. He knew the killers were not far away. It was either face them or jump from one cliff edge to another. Hobson's choice really. Martin decided to jump.

2 Choose one of the extracts and add 50 words to it. Try to move the story into the 'falling action' part of the structure.

Apply your skills

3 Plan the five-part plot of an exciting action story. Look back at your list of key events from a film or book to remind yourself of the *type* of events that happen in each part.

4 Now write the climax of your story. Use the extracts above to give you some ideas about how to make it exciting and interesting.

5 Write the beginning and resolution to your story.

Check your progress

Some progress

I can plan a simple story with a fitting start and finish.

Good progress

I can use the five-part narrative structure to organise a story.

Excellent progress

I can use and adapt the five-part narrative structure to organise my writing effectively.

Make your ending link back to your opening

Learning objectives
- link your conclusion to your opening
- argue and inform with facts.

You should try to link your conclusion back to your introduction, especially when writing arguments. This will remind your reader of your *purpose* and return to the key points made in your introduction.

Getting you thinking

In pairs, read this piece of argument writing.

Would you really like to be a Victorian child?

A lot of people think the past was something wonderful: the good old days, when things were better. Well, think again!

If you were lucky enough to stay at home you would probably have had to care for your younger brothers and sisters. Children as young as four or five were left in the house to look after their siblings while their parents worked.

Some boys were made to work as chimney sweeps. They were chosen because they were agile as well as small. These boys had to work in hot, dark, cramped conditions. Most boys scraped their legs, elbows and knees as they climbed up inside the chimney. They had to have their flesh hardened by rubbing it with salt water.

Those who went to school fared little better. Teachers regularly used the cane. Some teachers chose thin canes because they hurt more. The teacher would hit pupils hard and the slender cane would rebound and hit the pupil again. So if the teacher hit a boy once, the boy got two strokes!

Some naughty pupils were put in the stocks and left there. Some schools had a basket called the cage. Pupils were put in the cage and it was raised by rope until it almost reached the classroom ceiling. The class continued with the pupil left in the cage.

So you'd really like to be a Victorian, would you? Personally, I'd rather be growing up in the 21st century.

1 What do you notice about the opening and the ending of the article?

How does it work?

The *opening* usually tells the reader what the article is about and establishes its purpose.

The *middle* part moves from general to specific points. These paragraphs deal with different aspects of the argument, offering evidence to support it.

The *conclusion* should link back to the introduction.

Now you try it

2 Plan a letter to the author of this article in which you argue that being a child now is worse than being a child in Victorian times.

Plan for four or five paragraphs. Think about

- how you will introduce the topic
- how you will make your letter persuasive
- staying focused on your topic
- providing evidence to elaborate on your point
- linking the conclusion back to your original point.

> **Top tip**
>
> Letters often end with a 'call to action', telling the reader what the writer wants them to do.

Apply your skills

3 Use your IT skills to draft and finally write up your letter.

Checklist for success

- ✔ Put your address in the top right-hand corner.
- ✔ Put the date underneath it.
- ✔ Begin with 'Dear ...'.
- ✔ End with 'Yours sincerely' when writing to someone you know by name and 'Yours faithfully' when you have used 'Dear Sir/Madam' at the start.

Check your progress

Some progress

I can write an introduction and conclusion, which may be linked.

Good progress

I can write an effective conclusion that may refer back to my introduction.

Excellent progress

I can write an introduction that signals the direction of my letter and an effective conclusion that links back.

Check your progress

Some progress

- [ ] I can organise ideas in a logical sequence.
- [ ] I can write an effective opening.
- [ ] I can use some pictures, headings and colour to present my work effectively.
- [ ] I can identify the main points in a text.
- [ ] I can organise a simple story with a suitable beginning and ending.
- [ ] I can link my ending to my opening.

Good progress

- [ ] I can structure my work clearly and show links between my ideas.
- [ ] I can develop my ideas across a piece of writing.
- [ ] I can use sentences, paragraphs and presentational devices for effect.
- [ ] I can summarise the main points from a text.
- [ ] I can use the five-part structure to plan a story.
- [ ] I can use facts to argue and inform.

Excellent progress

- [ ] I can skilfully control the organisation of my writing.
- [ ] I can develop and link my ideas to write cohesively.
- [ ] I can present texts imaginatively to suit my purpose and audience.
- [ ] I can adapt key information to suit my purpose.
- [ ] I can use and adapt the five-part structure to organise my writing effectively.
- [ ] I can write a well-developed and linked series of paragraphs to argue and inform.

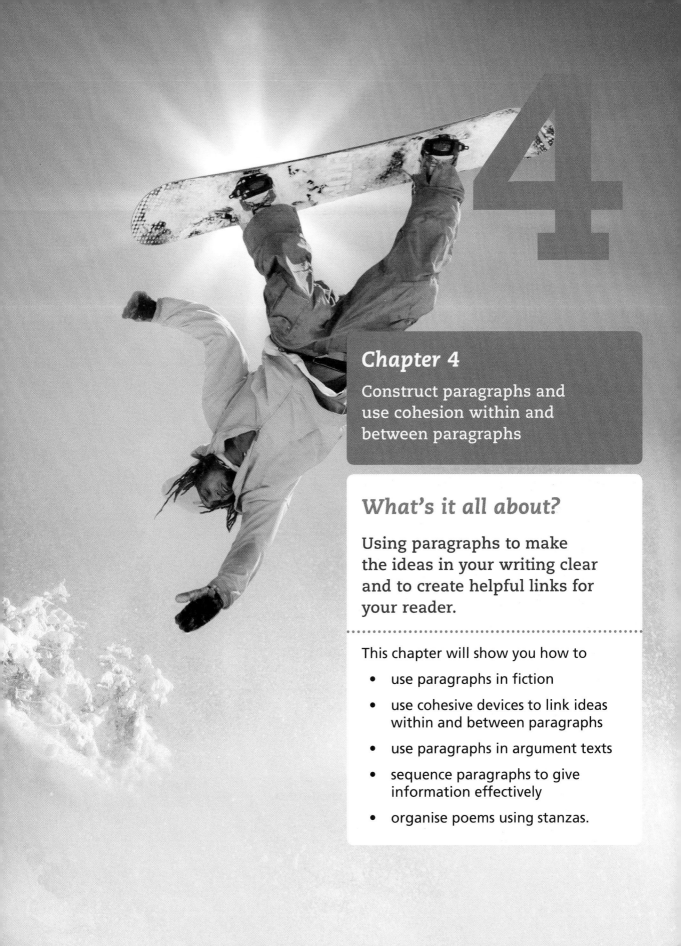

Chapter 4

Construct paragraphs and use cohesion within and between paragraphs

What's it all about?

Using paragraphs to make the ideas in your writing clear and to create helpful links for your reader.

This chapter will show you how to

- use paragraphs in fiction
- use cohesive devices to link ideas within and between paragraphs
- use paragraphs in argument texts
- sequence paragraphs to give information effectively
- organise poems using stanzas.

Use paragraphs in fiction

Learning objective

- understand how to begin a new paragraph in a story.

When writing fiction, such as a novel or short story, writers use paragraphs to help the reader follow the events.

Getting you thinking

Read this extract from the novel *Thursday's Child*. Harper's brother Tin has been caught in a mudslide and Harper is discussing this with her father.

'I didn't mean to let Tin get caught in a mudslide. I told him not to go near the water, I told him it wasn't safe. It was just an accident, Da. Audrey twisted my ear.'

'Hurt?'

I nodded sombrely. Da wiped his hair from his eyes.

'She was wrong to do that to your ear. Nobody can do anything about mud. It's one of those things that has a will of its own.'

I knew he was remembering being a soldier: Da said that in the war a whole country had changed into mud. The muddy country had **suctioned** down entire bodies of men and horses and no one saw a hair of them again. Da said that the soldiers would dig and dig frantically, **spurred on** by **gargling** screams, but the mud had a teasing nature and would suck its captive deeper just as the shovels were finding him, just as hands were reaching to clasp.

Thursday's Child by Sonya Hartnett

Glossary

suctioned: sucked

spurred on: urged on

gargling: choking with liquid mud (gargling means to rinse your throat with liquid)

1 With a partner, decide why the writer has started each new paragraph in this extract.

How does it work?

There are several reasons for starting a new paragraph in a story. It can show

- a change of *speaker*

- a change of *place* (this could be a small shift such as a person having walked into a house, or a huge shift such as the action switching to an astronaut on the moon)

- a change of *time* (when the action shifts forwards or backwards in time – this could be a minute or thousands of years!)

- a change of *topic*.

Now you try it

2 Read this extract from the same novel and decide where the paragraph breaks should go.

> From my place lying on the floor before the fire, I did not need to look up to know Da's eyes had darted to me. 'It was Tin, Mam,' I said listlessly. 'Ah,' Da exclaimed, and his hand slapped the table. 'What do you mean it was Tin?' 'Harper, enough!' I crooked my neck to peer at him. 'We have to tell, Da. People are asking.'

Apply your skills

3 Now write your own one-page short story. Remember to start a new paragraph whenever there is a change of speaker, place or time.

Your story could be about

- a grandfather comforting his grandchild who has fallen over and is hurt (he might reflect on his own childhood, when he was hurt in a farming accident)

- a war hero watching his grandchildren play a war game (he might tell them about his real war experience).

Check your progress

Some progress

I can start a new paragraph whenever dialogue is used.

Good progress

I can start new paragraphs when the action shifts.

Excellent progress

I can use new paragraphs when there is a change of speaker, place and time.

Use cohesive devices to link ideas within and between paragraphs

Learning objective
- use cohesive devices.

It is important to link ideas within and across paragraphs. This helps your reader understand how your ideas connect and develop.

Getting you thinking

Read this account of the execution of King Charles I.

> We built a scaffold in Westminster.
>
> 30th January 1649. A cold morning. Charles was trembling. 'With c-cold, not f-fear,' he said. He asked for a second shirt.
>
> He dressed himself neatly in his two shirts, not a hair out of place. He stared at the block. He stopped stammering.
>
> I said, 'Cut off his head with the crown upon it!'
>
> He lay down over the low block. A few grey hairs strayed out from his white cap. He tucked them back up neatly.
>
> I raised my head to the axeman. 'Do it boldly, Brandon!'
>
> 'Oliver, no!' begged Fairfax.
>
> The blade came down.
>
> *Cromwell's Talking Head* by Gareth Calway

1 With a partner, discuss how the writer creates links between the sentences and connections between the paragraphs, including the sections of speech.

How does it work?

The writer builds each paragraph from the initial idea that Charles is going to get his head chopped off. To create links, the writer uses the following methods.

- *repeated structures* ('He dressed' 'He stared' 'He tucked')

- **pronouns** such as 'he' to refer back to the character already named

- *linking the end back to the start* – the final paragraph refers back to the scaffold of the first paragraph and completes the action begun there.

Glossary

pronouns: words that are used instead of nouns (he, she, it, they, we, I and you)

Now you try it

Look at these ideas for a short story about Oliver Cromwell's first meeting with Charles I when Oliver was a young boy.

Oliver thought how short the king was.

As a baby, Oliver was stolen from his cradle by a monkey and taken up on a roof.

Oliver used to dream about meeting the king.

The monkey brought Oliver safely back to the ground.

Oliver saw a boil on the back of the king's neck as he left.

The king was wearing a fine lace collar and had sparkling rings on his fingers.

Everyone in the house panicked.

The king laughed when he heard about Oliver's monkey adventure.

Beds and blankets were placed on the ground in case the monkey threw him down.

The king entered and everyone bowed.

2 Divide the ideas into paragraphs. Which ideas would you group together in one paragraph? Rearrange the paragraphs so that the last one links back to the first.

3 Now write the first paragraph of your story.

Apply your skills

4 Using the linking techniques you have explored, write up the full story. Remember to *plan in paragraphs*.

Checklist for success

- ✔ Use pronouns for nouns you have already used.

- ✔ Use time connectives such as 'then', 'until' and 'after' to link paragraphs and order events.

- ✔ Redraft, edit out any 'padding' and finally proofread for publication!

Check your progress

Some progress
I can recognise cohesive devices.

Good progress
I can recognise and use cohesive devices in sentences and paragraphs.

Excellent progress
I can recognise and create cohesive devices throughout my texts.

Use paragraphs in argument texts

Learning objective

• order and link paragraphs into an argument.

Paragraphs need to be ordered in a clear and logical way, especially when writing texts that argue a point of view.

Getting you thinking

With a partner, read this essay exploring the arguments for and against the idea of setting a curfew for teenagers under 17.

In modern Britain, we experience all sorts of crime. Many people believe that it is possible to cut down on crime. It has been suggested that any teenager from the age of 13 to 16 should not be allowed out of their homes after 9.30pm until 7am the next morning – unless they are with a parent or guardian.

An argument for this idea is that teenagers are very likely to be involved in crimes such as car theft, car vandalism, general vandalism and low-level nuisance, such as 'knock and run'. Most of this sort of crime takes place at night. If teenagers were made to stay at home, these crimes would end.

However, the proposal would stop teenagers from joining safe and organised activities and events. It would also stop some law-abiding teenagers from doing their newspaper or milk rounds early in the morning.

Equally, though, in parts of the USA crime *has* been reduced by introducing curfews for teenagers. There are parts of Britain where teenage crime and nuisance is a problem, so something has to be done about it! There needs to be a curfew, but it might be better to impose it on children aged 10 to 14. After the age of 14, teenagers should be responsible for their own actions. Also, teenage crime isn't a problem in every part of the country. Perhaps local councils should have a curfew system that they think will work in their area.

1 Identify the main point made in each paragraph.

2 Label each paragraph as either *for* or *against* the argument.

3 Discuss what the writer's conclusion is.

How does it work?

The first paragraph is the *introduction*.

The second paragraph sets out the arguments *for the proposal*.

The third paragraph sets out arguments *against the proposal*.

The fourth paragraph *concludes* the piece.

Now you try it

Think about the following proposal:

> The driving age should be lowered to 14.

4 Plan your own argument essay. Think about each paragraph.

- What information will go where?

- When will you start a new paragraph (you may wish to switch between different points of view, for example)?

- Conclude with your own viewpoint.

Apply your skills

5 Now draft your essay, paying special attention to the *links* between paragraphs. Make these links logical so that the argument moves forward to the conclusion. Use some of the connectives in the table below.

However	Similarly	Alternatively
In the same way	In contrast	On one hand
In the first place	First	Nevertheless
Secondly	Equally	Moreover

Finally, proofread for mistakes and look for ways of improving your argument.

Check your progress

Some progress

I can plan the order of paragraphs in my essay.

Good progress

I can order paragraphs in a logical way in my argument, using connectives.

Excellent progress

I can use a clear approach and a variety of linking techniques to develop an argument.

Sequence paragraphs to give information effectively

Learning objective

- write information sheets using paragraphs.

Some writing is meant to *inform*, so that the reader ends up understanding a subject. When writing to inform, you need to set out your paragraphs in a logical order to present facts and processes in an easy-to-follow way.

Getting you thinking

Read this advice sheet about snowboarding.

Snowboarding can be a dangerous sport. It is not a good idea to be launched down a slope by some well-meaning but reckless friend who cheerfully shouts out instructions as you lurch dangerously near a cliff edge. It is much better to have proper lessons from a qualified snowboard instructor.

With such an instructor at a recognised snowboard school, you will learn how to snowboard faster and more safely. You will be taught techniques such as the important skill of stopping by using the board (much better than smashing into a pine tree!)

Some people are frightened of starting lessons. Why are people frightened? The answer is that we're scared of the unknown. We allow our imaginations to take over. We don't know what being on a snowboard feels like. We wonder what will happen if we make mistakes. That's why we all need qualified instructors.

Snowboarding is most certainly a sideways sport. When snowboarders move down a slope, they lead with one foot. Left footers are known as regular or natural riders and right footers are called Goofies. Goofy, the Disney character, surfed right-footed! You will quickly learn which foot is your lead foot.

So why not book a lesson and find out if you're a Goofy? It's fun!

1 With a partner, create a flow chart showing the main point made in each paragraph.

How does it work?

The advice sheet is ordered by topic. Each paragraph is linked through content (various aspects of snowboarding) and through language: for example, referring back to things mentioned earlier ('Right footers are called Goofies. […] So why not […] find out it you're a Goofy?').

Now you try it

2 In pairs, re-read the advice sheet.

a) Do you think it is well written?

b) Do you think the writer has missed out any important information? If so, what?

c) Look at the first paragraph – is it too long, too short or just right? Give reasons for your answer.

d) The information is in five paragraphs. To produce a more flowing piece of writing, could any of the paragraphs be combined? If so, which ones?

e) What do you notice about the length of the final paragraph? Is it an effective 'call to action'?

Apply your skills

3 Think of a sport or leisure activity you know well. Bullet-point your ideas or use a spider diagram to plan an advice sheet for teenagers wishing to take part in or learn about this activity. For example, if you choose to write about swimming, your plan might be:

- Introduction to swimming
- How to swim the breaststroke
- How to swim the crawl
- The dos and don'ts of swimming
- Life-saving techniques.

Think about the order (and length) of your paragraphs and then draft your advice sheet.

4 Now redraft your advice sheet, making the links between the paragraphs clearer.

Check your progress

Some progress »

I can use paragraphs to present facts about my chosen activity.

Good progress »»

I can sequence my paragraphs so my facts are presented in a way that is easy to understand.

Excellent progress »»»

I can present ordered paragraphs and I can redraft my advice sheet to improve it.

Organise poems using stanzas

Learning objective

• organise poems into stanzas.

Poetry has different rules from fiction. Instead of paragraphs, poems use groups of lines called stanzas.

Getting you thinking

Read this poem.

Seascape

My son had never seen the sea before,
I chose this perfect, heat stained August day.
He revelled in the treasures of the shore.

He took delight in everything he saw,
and paddled in the ripples of the bay.
My son had never seen the sea before.

He heard a seashell echo water's roar
and sifted sand from spade to bucket, play
he revelled in. The treasures of the shore,

of seaweed, crab and driftwood made a store,
a hoard for home. I told him not to stray.
My son had never seen the sea before.

I should have watched more carefully, made sure.
I should have known that he would creep away.
He revelled in the treasures of the shore.

I knew, before they gave up looking for
my child, the breakers gorged themselves on prey.
My son had never seen the sea before.
He revelled in the treasures of the shore.

Alison Chisholm

1. With a partner, write a sentence for each stanza explaining what it is about.

2. What regular patterns of rhyme, line and rhythm can you find?

3 Look at the repeated words and phrases, such as 'he' and 'I should have'. Why do you think the poet chose to repeat these words or phrases? How do the repeated lines mirror the action of the sea or tide?

How does it work?

Each stanza develops a new idea about the overall event the poem describes.

The stanzas have a regular rhythm and rhyme scheme. In each stanza the first and third lines rhyme, and every line of the poem has 10 syllables. This gives the poem a regular pace and a mood – a deceptively contented one, like the seascape. The repetitions of sound and ideas create a sense of being lulled remorselessly into danger.

Now you try it

4 Change the ending of the poem by altering the last two stanzas – apart from the last two lines.

- Link your new stanzas to the previous ones and the rest of the poem in rhyme, line and rhythm.

- Use the same rhyme scheme, and 10 syllables per line.

Apply your skills

5 Turn this *unformed* text into a poem of your own:

the mobile stops ringing the girl starts crying big tears like pearls drop the train passengers look away embarrassed when the train gets to the station everyone leaves not the girl she stares at the rain outside somewhere on the platform an MP3 is playing someone is singing a sad song for lovers in another town a boy dries his own tears turns up the radio turns off his mobile

a) Decide how many stanzas you will use, and explain to a partner why you have started each new stanza.

b) Choose where you will break each line, again explaining why you have made this decision.

Top tips

Before you start your poem, think up a list of rhyming words to include, related to the topic.

There is no right or wrong answer but think hard about *why* you are organising the poem in this way.

Check your progress

Some progress
I can write a simple poem, divided into stanzas.

Good progress
I can use stanzas to signal a change of topic in my poem.

Excellent progress
I can write a poem in stanzas chosen carefully to create effects or separate ideas.

Check your progress

Some progress

- ☐ I can support my main point with other sentences.
- ☐ I can link ideas between paragraphs.
- ☐ I can begin to vary sentences within a paragraph.
- ☐ I can recognise the use of stanzas in poetry.

Good progress

- ☐ I can use paragraphs to signal a change of subject, speaker, time or place.
- ☐ I can sequence paragraphs in a logical way.
- ☐ I can order paragraphs by topic or viewpoint.
- ☐ I can make logical links between paragraphs.
- ☐ I can recognise and write poetry using stanzas.

Excellent progress

- ☐ I can shape paragraphs quickly and coherently.
- ☐ I can order paragraphs logically and effectively.
- ☐ I can order paragraphs in fiction and argument texts by theme.
- ☐ I can create varied and clear bridges between paragraphs.
- ☐ I can write poetry using stanzas chosen carefully for effect or meaning.

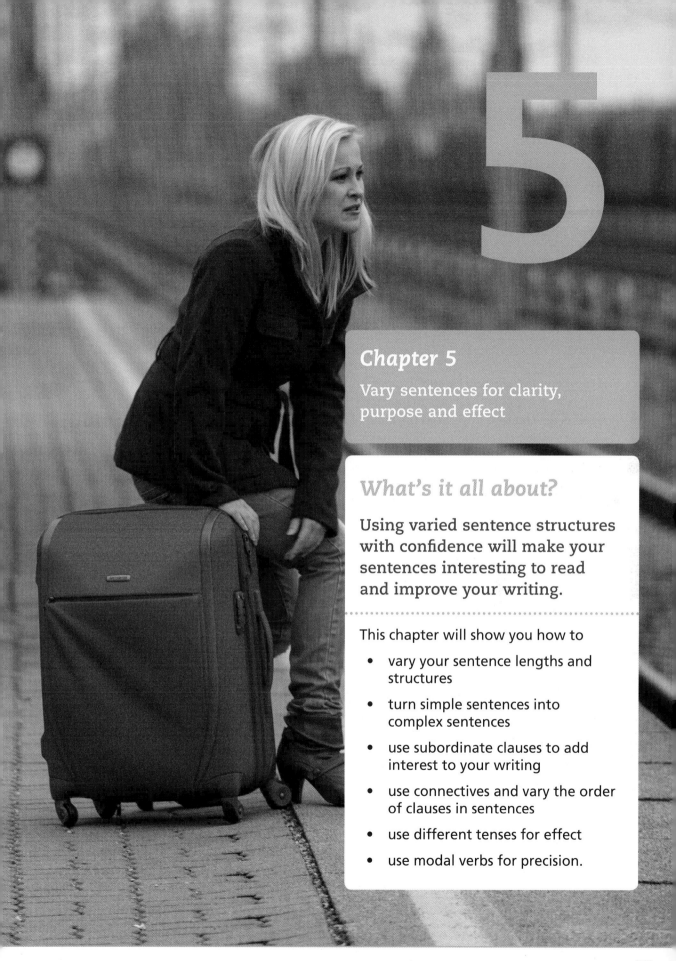

Chapter 5

Vary sentences for clarity,
purpose and effect

What's it all about?

Using varied sentence structures
with confidence will make your
sentences interesting to read
and improve your writing.

This chapter will show you how to

- vary your sentence lengths and
  structures
- turn simple sentences into
  complex sentences
- use subordinate clauses to add
  interest to your writing
- use connectives and vary the order
  of clauses in sentences
- use different tenses for effect
- use modal verbs for precision.

Vary your sentence lengths and structures

Learning objective
- think about sentence length and structure for effect.

A short simple sentence can give emphasis or deliver a shock or surprise in your writing. A longer sentence can build up tension and drama.

Getting you thinking

The Old Curiosity Shop was amazingly popular in Victorian times. People wept when they read about the death of its child heroine, Little Nell.

> She was dead. No sleep so beautiful and calm, so free from trace of pain, so fair to look upon. She seemed a creature fresh from the hand of God, and waiting for the breath of life, not one who had lived and suffered death. [...]
>
> She was dead. Dear, gentle, patient, noble Nell was dead. [...]
>
> Where were the traces of her early cares, her sufferings, and fatigues? All gone. Sorrow was indeed dead in her, but peace and perfect happiness were born; imaged in her tranquil beauty and profound repose.
>
> She was dead, and past all help, or need of it.
>
> *The Old Curiosity Shop* by Charles Dickens

1 Why you think readers responded so emotionally to Nell's death. Is it just the 'facts' of what happens, or is it something to do with *how* it is written?

How does it work?

This passage is built around a repeated short, simple sentence that has great force ('She was dead'). Dickens extends this by adding adjectives to create an extended noun phrase ('Dear, gentle, patient, noble Nell'). He also uses powers of three.

Now you try it

2 Extend these short sentences by adding three adjectives to each.

   a) My ... grandfather fell and broke his hip.

   b) The ... dog was in dire need of a bath.

   c) The ... car was abandoned in a field.

Longer sentences can give the reader more information and build drama in a story.

3 Look at these simple sentences. Add another longer sentence that tells you more about the first. For example: 'Bolt won again! He took the gold medal in the 200m final!'

a) At last the weather broke. It…

b) We had won the lottery! We….

c) The dictator was dead! At last….

d) The holidays were here. We….

Apply your skills

Read this extract from another story by Charles Dickens. It describes a creepy house.

It was a **solitary** house, standing in a neglected garden. It was uninhabited, but had, within a year or two, been cheaply repaired to make it **habitable**; I say cheaply, because the work had been done in a surface manner, and was already decaying as to the paint and plaster. [...] It was much too closely and heavily shadowed by trees, and, in particular, there were six tall poplars before the front windows, which were excessively **melancholy**. It was easy to see that it was an avoided house – a house that nobody would take. And the natural **inference** was that it had the reputation of being a haunted house.

The Haunted House by Charles Dickens

Glossary

solitary: lonely or by itself

habitable: suitable to live in

melancholy: sad or depressing

inference: conclusion

4 Imagine that you explore this house. You find something shocking in an upstairs room.

a) Use long sentences to describe crossing the garden, pushing open the front door, exploring the downstairs rooms, climbing the stairs and then forcing open a locked bedroom.

b) Use very short sentences to reveal what is in the mysterious room.

c) Follow these with extended short sentences to add extra detail.

Check your progress

Some progress

I can sometimes vary the length and structure of sentences.

Good progress

I can vary my sentences to give them force and clarity.

Excellent progress

I can use varied sentences for effect and to add extra detail.

Turn simple sentences into complex sentences

Learning objective

• use complex sentences in your writing.

Simple sentences are sometimes exactly right but to make your writing more varied you should try to use **compound** and **complex sentences**.

Getting you thinking

John loves Sir Arthur Conan Doyle's story *The Hound of the Baskervilles*. His favourite part is where Sherlock Holmes and Dr Watson watch as the ghostly Hound appears out of the fog.

Read John's version of this episode:

> We waited. The fog began to clear. We had no time to hide. The great Hound appeared. It was shocking. It was as big as a pony. Its face and terrible mouth glowed green in the darkness. We were shocked. We did not fire our pistols at once. The creature raced onwards after Sir Henry.

His teacher suggested improvements:

> As we waited, the fog began to clear. Before we had time to hide, the great Hound appeared. It was shocking because it was as big as a pony and its face and terrible mouth glowed green in the darkness. Because we were shocked, we did not fire our pistols at once, while the creature raced onwards after Sir Henry.

1 Which passage sounds more interesting? How are the sentences in the second version different from the sentences in the first?

How does it work?

Look at the following words. They are called *subordinating conjunctions*.

after	although	because	before	if
so	since	though	unless	until
when	while	where	wherever	as

Glossary

compound sentences: sentences made up of two or more main clauses (parts that would make sense as sentences on their own)

complex sentences: sentences made up of a main clause and a subordinate clause or clauses (parts that would not make sense as sentences on their own)

Conjunctions allow you to add information to a simple sentence to turn it into a complex sentence.

Now you try it

2 Add to the sentences below to create four complex sentences.

a) Although it was raining, . . .

b) When I was younger, . . .

c) Because he was bad tempered, . . .

d) Unless we can think of a plan, . . .

> **Top tip**
>
> When using a conjunction at the start of a sentence, place a comma after the first part of the sentence: 'Although I had a heavy cold, I still ran the race.'

You can also make your sentences more interesting by changing the word order. The extra information you add can come at the start, middle or end of the sentence.

We are doomed, unless we can think of a plan.

Unless we can think of a plan, we are doomed.

We are, unless we can think of a plan, doomed.

Notice where the commas are placed in each example.

3 Change the word order of the following sentences.

a) Until the last minute, I thought Blackburn would win.

b) When the going gets tough, the tough get going.

c) Before I met you, life was dull.

Apply your skills

Here is another passage by John about the *Hound of the Baskervilles*. The Hound finally attacks Sir Henry Baskerville.

> The huge black creature was leaping down the track. The fog cleared. It was now bright moonlight. Holmes and I both fired together. The creature gave a hideous howl. He bounded onward. We saw Sir Henry looking back. The Hound knocked him down. It attacked his throat.

4 Rewrite this paragraph

- adding detail and imagining what happens next
- turning simple sentences into complex sentences
- trying out different word orders in your sentences.

Check your progress

Some progress
I can use some variety of sentence structure.

Good progress
I can vary my sentence structures using some complex sentences.

Excellent progress
I can effectively control my use of complex sentences.

Use subordinate clauses to add interest to your writing

Learning objectives

- identify main and subordinate clauses
- use clauses with who/whom, that/which and whose.

A complex sentence contains a *main clause* and one or more *subordinate clauses*. The subordinate clauses may be introduced by *relative pronouns*.

Getting you thinking

A *clause* is a group of words that contains

- a *subject* (someone or something that is doing or being something)
- a *predicate* (the other words in a clause – this must always include a verb).

Volunteers collected the litter after a festival.

predicate

subject

1 Look at these sentences about the novelist Jane Austen. Copy them out and underline the subject in each, then the verb, then the predicate (which includes the verb).

a) Jane Austen wrote her famous novels in the early 19th century.

b) 2013 marked the bicentenary of the publication of *Pride and Prejudice*.

c) This great novel inspired a very popular television adaptation in 1995.

d) Funny rom-coms, like *Clueless*, are based on Jane Austen's stories.

e) Chawton, Jane Austen's former home in Hampshire, receives thousands of visitors.

How does it work?

Simple sentences contain only one clause.

Compound sentences are made up of two or more clauses of equal strength, joined by *coordinating conjunctions* (such as 'and', 'or', 'but', 'yet').

Clueless was based on Jane Austen's novel *Emma* and starred Alicia Silverstone.

(clause one) (conjunction) (clause two)

Sometimes one clause is weaker than the other. The weaker one is called a *subordinate clause*. The stronger one is the *main clause*. Together, the clauses make a *complex sentence*.

Pride and Prejudice, which was published in 1813, is Austen's most famous novel.

(main clause) (subordinate clause) (main clause)

The subordinate clause usually just adds information to the main clause. The main clause would still work without it:

Pride and Prejudice is Austen's most famous novel.

Subordinate clauses that give us more information about people or things are introduced by *relative pronouns* such as 'who', 'whom', 'that', 'which' and 'whose'.

> **Top tip**
>
> Subordinate clauses that modify the subject are called *relative clauses*. They often use relative pronouns to refer back to the subject.

Now you try it

2 The sentences in the first column of the table below are missing their subordinate clauses. Write them out, adding the subordinate clause. You will also need to add commas, as in the example below:

My brother often got into trouble at school.

My brother, who was very talkative, often got into trouble at school.

Simple sentences	Subordinate clauses
Our puppy chews almost everything.	which is very playful
Amanda Higgins always gets her homework done.	whose mother is a teacher
The overweight horse is not a champion.	which ate too much hay

Apply your skills

3 Write a short description of a group of people that you know (a team, a group, friends in a class, family members). Include some sentences with subordinate clauses, introduced by relative pronouns.

Here are some useful phrases to help you:

whose nickname is… / who likes to… / whom I saw once… / who has a dog which…

Check your progress

Some progress
I can include some subordinate clauses in my description.

Good progress
I can use subordinate clauses introduced by relative pronouns.

Excellent progress
I can write a lively description using simple, compound and complex sentences.

Use connectives and vary the order of clauses in sentences

Learning objective

- link and vary the order of the clauses in your sentences.

If you can link and order your sentences well, it will make your writing more coherent.

Getting you thinking

Compare these two paragraphs about video games.

> I love playing video games. My brother detests them. My sister also hates everything about them. I can never share my enjoyment with my family.

> In my spare time, I love playing video games. By contrast, my brother detests them. Similarly, my sister hates everything about them. Therefore I can never share my enjoyment with my family.

 1 Which version sounds better? What effect do the extra words in the second version have on the sentences? Discuss this in pairs.

Top tip

Connectives can be used at the start, in the middle or at the end of a sentence.

How does it work?

Connectives like these are useful to link or relate separate sentences, especially in formal writing:

so that	similarly	by contrast	next	consequently	finally
thus	therefore	for example	above all	in conclusion	however

No answer has been received. Consequently, this country is at war.

Some marriages end in divorce. Many, however, are happy and long-lasting.

You can also blend sentences together with connectives. Experiment with the order of your sentences to make them more forceful or to stress particular information.

> 'I am sending you to prison for twenty years, despite your previous good record and difficult family life.'

The order could be changed to focus on the prison sentence:

> 'Despite your previous good record and difficult family life, I am sending you to prison for twenty years.'

2 Join these pairs of sentences using connectives.

   a) I am quite tall. My brother is surprisingly short.

   b) This film is exciting and has memorable characters and amazing settings. It is totally brilliant.

   c) The evidence is overwhelming. I find you guilty of this awful crime.

3 Vary the order of these sentences by placing the connective phrase in different places.

   a) Out there in the wilderness, the children were waiting.

   b) Without your support and generous donations, the High Cross Animal Centre could not survive.

Apply your skills

Look at this information sheet about J.K. Rowling.

Joanne Rowling was twenty-five when she first thought up Harry Potter.

The Harry Potter idea came to her on a train from Manchester to London in 1990.

She invented the school of wizards in her head. She then wrote her first notes in a cheap notebook.

She planned seven books about Harry from the start, one for each of his school years.

The first was written in an Edinburgh café.

She did secretarial work to earn money while she prepared the first book.

She sent an outline and three chapters to the Christopher Little Literary Agency.

Bryony Evans, an editorial assistant at Little's, spotted the magic of the book.

Several publishers refused Harry Potter. Bloomsbury published it in 1997.

4 Use the facts above, and the techniques you have learned, to write a short biography of the author of the *Harry Potter* books.

You might want to find additional information on the internet.

Check your progress

Some progress

I can use some simple connectives in my biography.

Good progress

I can vary the order of clauses in my sentences.

Excellent progress

I can link sentences with connectives and vary the order of clauses for effect.

Use different tenses for effect

Learning objective

- understand and use the different tenses of verbs.

Tenses change the form of **verbs**. It is important to know how to use tenses so you can create different effects and keep your writing interesting.

Glossary

verbs: words that tell us about *actions* ('hit', 'run', 'cook') or *states of being* ('seem', 'am')

Getting you thinking

You are writing a story set in Victorian times about the mysterious Lady Audley, who has a strange secret in her life. In your first draft, you use the *past tense*:

> Brilliant moonlight allowed me to find the meeting place in the tree-shaded lime walk. My feet rustled the fallen leaves. A dog was barking nervously. An owl shrieked. Across the moonlit lawn, a dark figure, wrapped in a cloak, advanced to meet me. I could see her frosty breath in the cold air. I whispered a greeting. Would she finally tell me about her mysterious secret?

1 This would be more dramatic in the *present tense*. Pick out all the verbs and change them from past to present (for example, 'allowed' becomes 'allows').

How does it work?

Tense shows us the time of the verb (past, present or future:

Past	Present	Future
I saw	I see	I shall/will see

There are different forms of the past tense:

Present perfect	Past perfect
I have seen	I had seen

Some tenses are *progressive*. The action or state goes on for some time:

Past	Present	Future
I was eating	I am eating	I shall/will be eating

Progressive tenses are formed with *participles*, which are parts of verbs.

A *present participle* ends in *-ing*: going

You must add an *auxiliary verb* to a present participle to make it into a complete verb:

> I am going to the cinema on Friday.
> auxiliary + participle = complete verb

It is the same with the *past progressive*:

> I was going to visit my granny.
> auxiliary + participle = complete verb

Now you try it

Sport really comes alive in the present tense. We like to see what is happening in the match NOW! Here is a football commentary in the past tense.

2 Rewrite this text using the present tense.

> Smith flicked the ball across the goal mouth. Diaz, the defender, completely missed it. Rogers raced into the box and nodded the ball down to Leroy. A lovely back-heel sent the ball into the back of the net. GOAL!

Apply your skills

Robert Southey, a 19th-century poet, wrote a poem for his children about the waterfalls of Lodore in the Lake District. He did it all with present participles to show how the water rushed down.

The Cataract of Lodore

Retreating and beating and meeting and sheeting,
Delaying and straying and playing and spraying,
Advancing and prancing and glancing and dancing,
Recoiling, turmoiling and toiling and boiling,
And rushing and flushing and brushing and gushing…

Robert Southey

3 Write a description of pupils leaving school when the afternoon bell rings, using as many present participles as you can. Divide them with the conjunction 'and' or commas.

Check your progress

Some progress
I can get most verb forms and tenses right.

Good progress
I can use verb forms and tenses correctly in more complicated sentences.

Excellent progress
I can use verb forms and tenses accurately and for strong effect in varied sentence patterns.

Use modal verbs for precision

Learning objective
- understand and use modal verbs.

Modals are a type of auxiliary (helping) verb. They combine with other verbs to express levels of certainty or possibility. Modals can also help make your meaning more subtle and precise.

Getting you thinking

Look at these sentences.

The train is late.	The train will be late.	The train may be late.

The first sentence is definite: the train is late *now*.

The second sentence is also definite about a *future event*.

The last sentence is less certain. There is a *possibility about a future event*.

1 Which are the modal verbs in the three statements below? What are the differences among these sentences?

a) They are waiting for you.

b) They will wait for you.

c) They might not wait for you.

How does it work?

Modal verbs are auxiliaries (helping verbs). The main modal verbs are

can	could	might	may	ought to
should	would	shall ('ll)	shan't	will
won't (will not)	can't (cannot)	must	mustn't	

Modals join with other verbs:

I must go	you ought to see	they could be
I can take	he might miss	she must see

The verbs are changed to express

- what is possible: 'Maybe you *can* see what I mean.'
- what may happen in the future: 'John *should* get home at nine.'
- what you need to do: 'You *ought to* see a dentist at once.'

Now you try it

Look at the ideas on the right for a visit to Sydney.

Now here are some verbs:

enjoy	explore	photograph	go on
visit	tour	relax on	experience

Opera House

boat trip around the harbour

Sydney Harbour Bridge

surfing on Bondi beach

shops in Oxford Street

the Royal Botanic gardens

Sydney Zoo

2 Using these ideas, write an email to a friend who is about to visit Sydney, suggesting some things that he or she could or should do. Add modal auxiliaries to each verb.

Apply your skills

June is a busy time at school, with exam preparation going on. Your uncle and his family are visiting from Australia. They want to go on the London Eye, and they invite you to take a day off school to join them. The head teacher is very strict about attendance but you decide to write him a letter, asking for permission to miss a day.

3 Compose a short, polite letter, using plenty of positive modal verbs from the table opposite.

4 Then write the head teacher's grim reply, this time using negative modal verbs.

Check your progress

Some progress 〉〉

I can pick out some modal forms in writing.

Good progress 〉〉

I understand how modal verbs affect tone in my letters.

Excellent progress 〉〉〉

I can write both letters using positive and negative modals to vary the tone.

Check your progress

Some progress

- [ ] I can check simple sentences.
- [ ] I can make compound sentences using conjunctions.
- [ ] I can try out complex sentences.
- [ ] I understand how subordinate clauses work.

Good progress

- [ ] I can understand main and subordinate clauses.
- [ ] I can use various kinds of subordinate and relative clauses.
- [ ] I can think about sentence length, structure and word order.
- [ ] I can use connectives to relate sentences.
- [ ] I can understand and use various forms and tenses of verbs.

Excellent progress

- [ ] I can vary sentence patterns for emphasis and effect.
- [ ] I can use conjunctions and other connectives to vary sentence patterns.
- [ ] I can use simple, compound and complex sentences to suit particular purposes.
- [ ] I can understand and use varied verb forms and tenses, and use them for effect.

Chapter 6

Write with technical accuracy of syntax and punctuation in phrases, clauses and sentences

What's it all about?

Using speech marks, apostrophes, colons and semicolons accurately will improve your writing.

This chapter will show you how to

- use speech punctuation effectively
- use apostrophes for contraction in informal writing
- use apostrophes for possession
- use semicolons accurately
- use colons accurately
- use other forms of punctuation for effect.

Use speech punctuation effectively

Learning objective

- use correct punctuation and layout of written speech.

Spoken dialogue is an important part of fictional story writing. You should learn to present speech accurately and to use the correct punctuation.

Getting you thinking

With a partner, read this dialogue:

'I don't really like short stories,' said Sanjay. —— comma goes inside speech marks

—— full stop at the end of the sentence

'How many have you read?' asked Mr Baraka.

'A few,' Sanjay replied. 'They're just not very exciting. You never really get to know the characters.' —— full stop at end of first spoken sentence, followed by capital

'Not all short stories are like that. You should try Thomas Hardy's "The Withered Arm" or "The Signalman" by Charles Dickens. They can be really spine-tingling!' —— second line of speech returns to margin

'Great,' said Sanjay, 'I'll see if I can find them in the library.' —— commas because spoken sentence is broken

 Who is speaking in the fourth section of dialogue? How do you know?

How does it work?

Speech marks (also called inverted commas) go round the actual words of a speaker. Remember to

- use single speech marks
- start each new speaker in a new paragraph
- indent each new speaker 2 cm (handwriting) or one tab (computer) from the margin
- put any punctuation in the speech itself inside the speech marks
- use an ellipsis (...) or a dash (–) to indicate where a sentence is broken off
- use **synonyms** for 'says' and 'said'.

Top tip

For speech within speech, or for a quotation within a quotation, use double speech marks.

Glossary

synonyms: words that have almost the same meaning

Now you try it

2 Write out the rest of the conversation below, putting in the correct speech marks and punctuation.

> You'd probably like stories by H. G. Wells or Arthur Conan Doyle's Sherlock Holmes stories you'd certainly like Graham Greene's The Destructors or Daphne du Maurier's The Birds went on Mr Baraka

> I can't believe there are so many stories I've never even heard of cried Sanjay I like science fiction so maybe I'll start with H. G. Wells

Apply your skills

In Charles Dickens's story 'The Signalman', the narrator talks to a lonely signalman working on an isolated stretch of railway. He has seen a hooded figure waving and shouting by the mouth of a tunnel.

3 With a partner, read their conversation and look at the punctuation and layout. How does it add to the drama of the piece?

'Who is it?'

'I don't know. I never saw the face. The left arm is across the face and the right arm is waved – violently waved. This way.'

I followed his action with my eyes...

'One moonlight night,' said the man, 'I was sitting here when I heard a voice cry "Halloa! Below there!" I started up, looked from that door, and saw this someone else standing by the red light near the tunnel, waving as I just now showed you. The voice seemed hoarse with shouting, and it cried, "Look out! Look out!" I caught up my lamp, turned it on red, and ran towards the figure calling, "What's wrong? What has happened? Where?" I wondered at its keeping the sleeve across its eyes. I ran right up at it, and had my hand stretched out to pull the sleeve away, when it was gone.'

A rail crash in the tunnel happens soon afterwards. The ghost appears again and covers its face with both hands.

4 Write the conversation between the narrator and the signalman, explaining what happened on the second appearance. Follow the rules of speech punctuation.

Check your progress

Some progress
I can use some speech punctuation.

Good progress
I can write and punctuate written speech accurately.

Excellent progress
I can use accurate speech punctuation and can use synonyms to make my dialogue interesting.

Use apostrophes for contractions in informal writing

Learning objective

- use apostrophes to create an informal tone.

Contractions (short forms of words) are often used in informal writing, especially in speech. It is important to know when and how to write them correctly.

Getting you thinking

Contractions are short forms of words where one or more letters have been missed out. They are common in dialogue because we tend to run words together when we speak.

Contractions give your writing an informal tone, so you should avoid them in more formal writing.

1 With a partner, decide how you would write the contraction in each of these phrases:

are not	he would	it is	we will	they have
she had	they are	I had	he had	we are

Remember to think about which letters will be missing.

How does it work?

The rule is simple. To make a contraction, put the apostrophe in place of the missing letter or letters:

   aren't   he'd   it's   we'll   they've

Take care, though – not all contractions follow this rule.

- 'will not' changes to 'won't'
- 'shall not' changes to 'shan't'
- 'cannot' changes to 'can't'

You also see apostrophes for contraction in archaic (outdated) language in poems and plays:

   'twas (it was)   o'er (over)   'tis (it is)

Top tip

You need apostrophes in old forms that we still use (for example, 'o'clock'), but you don't need them in contractions that have become new words (for example, 'bus' and 'phone').

Now you try it

Look at this email from the organisers of a music festival.

To: Andrew Matthews
From: Cool Vibes Events
Subject: Sold Out

I am afraid the Cool Vibes Festival is sold out. We did not expect to have so much interest in tickets. We would have called you directly to confirm that your booking had been unsuccessful, but we cannot find a record of your telephone number. I will put your name on the reserve list for tickets in case we have any returns. You are welcome to contact me if you have any queries.

2 Using contractions, rewrite the email. Try to make it sound more informal.

Apply your skills

Three teenagers, Pete, Harry and Kamal, are the sole survivors of a shipwreck on a desert island. They sit on the beach, checking their resources and making plans.

They have these things:

shorts	a mobile phone but no charger!
rucksacks	a lighter (half-empty)
no food	one bottle of water
T-shirts	flip flops

The island has these features:

white sandy beaches	fruit trees	coconut trees
a warm climate	oysters and fish	wild pigs

3 Write a conversation they might have on the beach as they think about exploration and survival. Try to include the contractions of these phrases:

I shall	we are	we have	it is
you will	there is	it will	there is
it has	they are	I have	you are
we cannot	it would	we have not	where is

Check your progress

Some progress

I can get apostrophes right in some short forms of words.

Good progress

I can generally use apostrophes for short forms of words, especially in familiar language and speech.

Excellent progress

I can use apostrophes for contraction accurately to write a fluent conversation.

Use apostrophes for possession

Learning objective

- use apostrophes to show ownership.

Using possessive apostrophes correctly means that you can express your ideas more clearly and accurately.

Getting you thinking

Read this short passage:

> The girls were ready for the end-of-term prom. Alice's hair was beautifully cut, Jayda's necklace sparkled in the lights, Indira's green evening dress suited her perfectly and Adeena's high heels made her walk elegantly. Jayda's father arrived with the huge black limousine that was part of the family's private hire fleet. The girls' great evening was about to begin!

1 Find seven *owner* words and seven things *owned* – as shown by possessive apostrophes.

How does it work?

The rules of the possessive apostrophe are simple:

- Put 's or ' on the end of the owner word.
- For **singular** words add 's.
- For **plural** words ending in -s add ' only: ladies' toilets.

For most singular owner nouns just add 's:

- Cathy's bike
- London's streets and squares
- my sister's boyfriend.

Look out for *owner names ending in -s*. You will see them ending in 's or just ':

- Dickens' novels or Dickens's novels.

Glossary

singular: one

plural: more than one

The same applies to nouns ending in -s:

- bus's or bus' wheels.

For plural owner words ending in -s, just add ':

- boys' football match (several boys)
- grandparents' anniversary

Words with -en plural endings also take 's:

- men's snooker club
- children's literature.

Now you try it

2 Here are 10 owner words and 10 things owned. Put them together, using the possessive apostrophe correctly.

Hopkins	poems	James	bank account
two weeks	holiday	Mercedes	engine
babies	prams	its	collar
fortnight	time	men	shoe shop
uncle	birthday	cars	parking spaces

3 Compare your answers with a partner. Did you agree?

Apply your skills

4 Write an email to a friend. Because this is informal, it is fine to use contractions. In your email, describe the house of a family that you know and recently visited. Include some of the following details about the house:

Sitting room: large, ugly wallpaper, battered furniture, smell of dogs, very old TV, pictures painted by father.

Dad (Jerry): studio: piles of canvases, table covered with paints, art posters.

Twins (Laura and Gemma) (13): bedroom: bunk beds, piles of soft toys, *Hunger Games* poster.

James (17): bedroom: white painted walls, new laptop, clothes lying on floor, dirty dinner plates, desk covered with folders, Batman poster.

Check your progress

Some progress

I can sometimes get apostrophes for possession right.

Good progress

I can generally use possessive apostrophes correctly in an email.

Excellent progress

I can use apostrophes for possession accurately to write a clear and informal email.

Use semicolons accurately

Learning objective

- use semicolons for division or contrast.

Semicolons are used to divide items in a long list or to separate contrasting parts of a sentence.

Getting you thinking

In his novel *Barnaby Rudge*, Charles Dickens describes the Gordon riots in London in 1780. Here the mad crowd sets fire to an old house (the pile):

> The burning pile, revealing rooms and passages red hot, through gaps made in the crumbling walls; the fires that licked the outer bricks and stones, with their long forked tongues; the shining of the flames upon the villains who looked on and fed them; the roaring of the angry blaze; the living flakes the wind bore rapidly away and hurried on with, like a storm of fiery snow; [...] combined to form a scene never to be forgotten by those who saw it.
>
> *Barnaby Rudge* by Charles Dickens

1 Look at how Dickens uses semicolons here. Add two more long items to the list before the ellipses.

How does it work?

A semicolon (;) *divides*. It is used in two particular places:

- To divide longer items in a list, as in the extract above. You could use commas, but the semicolons make the sentence easier to follow. With a list like this you begin with a colon (:).

- To contrast two statements that are closely related.

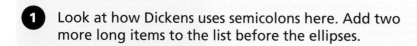

> Dogs are friendly but need constant attention; cats are independent and easy to manage.

These sentence patterns are useful in factual essays.

Now you try it

2 Look at the following pairs of contrasting ideas. For each idea, write a single sentence. Then put the two ideas into one sentence, using a semicolon to separate the statements.

primary school	secondary school
city	country
films	books
summer	winter
basketball	online game

Apply your skills

Rupert Brooke wrote this poem in 1914 to explain the little things that he enjoyed in life.

The Great Lover

These I have loved:
     White plates and cups, clean-gleaming,
Ringed with blue lines; and feathery, **faery** dust;
Wet roofs, beneath the lamp-light; the strong crust
Of friendly bread; and many-tasting food;
Rainbows; and the blue bitter smoke of wood;
And radiant raindrops couching in cool flowers;
And flowers themselves, that sway through sunny hours,
Dreaming of moths that drink them under the moon;
Then, the cool kindliness of sheets, that soon
Smooth away trouble; and the rough male kiss
Of blankets; grainy wood; live hair that is
Shining and free; blue-**massing** clouds; the keen
Unpassioned beauty of a great machine; [...]

Rupert Brooke

Glossary

faery: fairy

massing: gathering

Check your progress

Some progress
I can use semicolons in lists.

Good progress
I can use semicolons to contrast statements or to divide longer items in a list.

Excellent progress
I can use a full range of accurate punctuation including semicolons.

3 Write your own list poem about things you love or hate. Use the same punctuation pattern of a colon to introduce and semicolons to divide the items. Bring in details from your five senses.

Use colons accurately

Colons can be very useful to improve your writing, as long as you use them in the right places.

Getting you thinking

Read this short passage:

> Signs of autumn were increasing: leaves lay scattered on the lawn; spiders' webs, covered with dew, were easily visible; fallen apples, half-eaten by birds, lay under the trees; and the late-flowering roses let their petals fall.

1 Why are the semicolons used in this long sentence?

2 Why is the first clause ('Signs of autumn were increasing') different from the other parts of the sentence? What is the purpose of the colon after 'increasing'?

How does it work?

A colon is used to introduce a list of items.

- Start with an introductory statement, which should be a complete sentence.

- Then add your colon.

- The list, starting with a small letter, then follows.

> In the loft, I found relics of family history: old letters, faded photos, vinyl records, broken toys and dusty furniture.

— complete clause introduction
— colon
— list

A colon is also used in a sentence where **a** general statement is followed by more detailed evidence to explain or develop the idea. The explanation that follow it does not have to be long.

> Smith was the perfect footballer: he was untiring, passed well, evaded tackles easily, positioned himself cleverly and shot powerfully.

— general statement
— colon
— evidence

Here is a general statement:

> My closest friends are these people (Add a colon and a list of names.)

3 Now think of your own sentence like this, including a colon and a list.

Here is another general statement:

> I have one chief ambition in life (Add a colon and a singe phrase or clause.)

4 Now write your own statement, followed by a colon and a single explanation.

Apply your skills

Colons are also used in playscripts.

- Put the character's name in the margin (usually in capitals), followed by a colon.
- Put stage directions in brackets.
- Then write what the character says (you do not need to use speech marks)
- Start the next character's speech on a new line.

> **AVA:** *(sadly)* He's gone... and I'm afraid I'll never see him again.
>
> **JADE:** *(jumping up and hugging her friend)* London's not so far away. He'll be back. You'll see...

5 Create your own short playscript. Base it on the following situation or use your own idea. Try to include a list of items using colons.

> Anita (15) wants to go to the local nightclub with her friends. Her mum is worried and tries to reason with Anita. Her dad gets cross and refuses permission. Her older brother, Jay, just home from college, tries to keep the peace and promises his sister some sort of night out.

> **Top tip**
>
> The introductory statement before a colon should be a complete sentence. 'In the loft, I found:...' is not correct.)

Check your progress

Some progress »

I can use colons to introduce a list.

Good progress »

I can use colons to introduce a list or an explanation of a general statement, or in playscripts.

Excellent progress »»

I can use a full range of punctuation accurately, including colons.

Use other forms of punctuation for effect

Learning objective

- use important minor points of punctuation.

As well as punctuation such as speech marks, semicolons and colons, other types of punctuation can have particular impact in the right places.

Getting you thinking

Read this opening from an advert for people to work for a well-known charity:

> Want to make a difference? We need volunteers to work in our shops, help in our store-rooms and collect donations. You can help improve other people's lives – and you might even improve your own. What are you waiting for? Give us a call!

1 Apart from commas, full stops and question marks, two other types of punctuation are used here.

   a) What are they?

   b) Why have they been used?

Writers often use punctuation marks such as brackets and dashes to provide extra information, or asides. Look at this blog.

> To my shame, I have never done any voluntary work (unless you count loading the dishwasher at home) and it is something I am determined to put right. So my first day working in the Oxfam shop will be a big step in the right direction – but a nervous one, too!

2 What punctuation is used here?

How does it work?

In more informal writing, or when a sense of drama is needed, these punctuation marks can be very effective in creating the right tone. In the blog

- *brackets* are used to add a humorous detail (pairs of dashes could be used instead of brackets here)
- a *dash* is used to emphasise a new idea or slightly contrasting point about the writer's worries
- an *exclamation mark* emphasises the writer's nerves.

Now you try it

Read this light-hearted article about the same writer's first day working in a charity shop.

> My first day: what can I say? Well, there are lots of words I could use to describe it. 'Disaster' would be one of them. But suffice to say it didn't go well. Because it was a 'charity shop' I kept on giving things away for free. I'm not kidding. Duh. I think I may have got a little bit mixed up over the whole charity thing. The little old lady I was working with, who looked sweet and kind at least on the surface, gave me a right old telling off. I may be the first person to be sacked from an unpaid job.

3 Rewrite the article, improving it by using dashes, brackets and exclamation marks.

4 Compare your article with a partner's. Did you agree on where to put these punctuation features?

Apply your skills

5 Now write your own light-hearted blog/diary entry about a disastrous experience or event. You can base it on a real experience or make one up. Here are some suggestions:

- First day working in a busy café frequented by senior citizens.
- A day trip on a ferry during which the weather turns rough.
- A performance in a school play, talent show or assembly that goes horribly wrong.

Check your progress

Some progress

I can identify the use of other types of punctuation in texts and use at least one accurately.

Good progress

I can use dashes, brackets and exclamation marks to create different effects.

Excellent progress

I can use a full range of punctuation accurately and creatively.

Check your progress

Some progress

- [ ] I can punctuate and set out written speech.
- [ ] I know about apostrophes for short forms and for possession.
- [ ] I can use semicolons for division in lists.
- [ ] I can use bracketing commas.

Good progress

- [ ] I can use more complicated speech punctuation.
- [ ] I can use apostrophes accurately for contraction and possession.
- [ ] I can use semicolons accurately for division and contrast.
- [ ] I know when it is appropriate to use brackets and exclamation marks.

Excellent progress

- [ ] I understand the differences between direct and reported speech and use each one appropriately.
- [ ] I can use apostrophes for contraction appropriately when writing informally.
- [ ] I can use colons and semicolons appropriately and accurately throughout my writing.
- [ ] I can use a wide range of punctuation for effect, including brackets, dashes and exclamation marks.

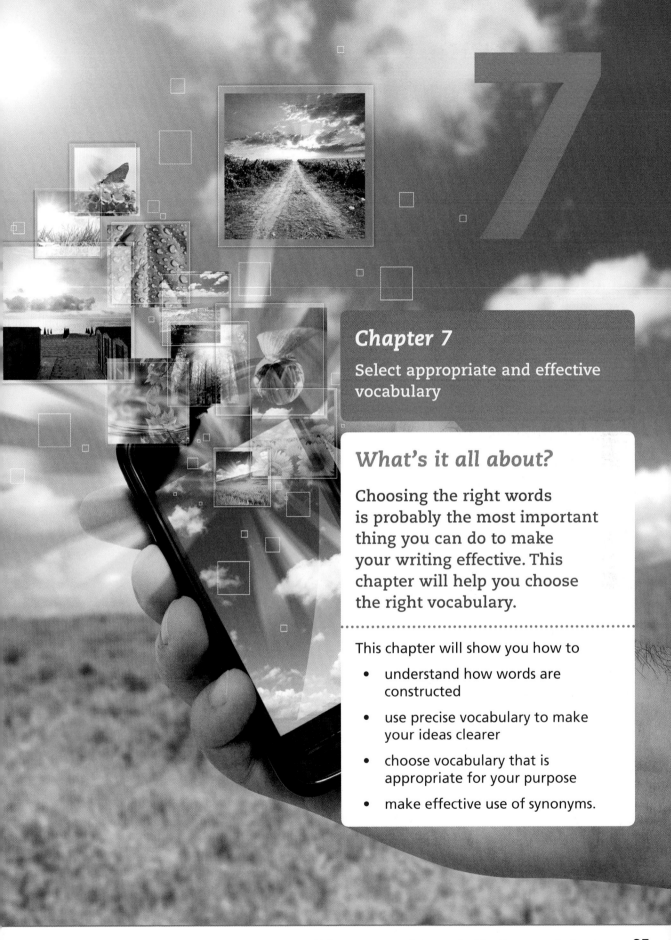

Chapter 7

Select appropriate and effective vocabulary

What's it all about?

Choosing the right words is probably the most important thing you can do to make your writing effective. This chapter will help you choose the right vocabulary.

This chapter will show you how to

- understand how words are constructed
- use precise vocabulary to make your ideas clearer
- choose vocabulary that is appropriate for your purpose
- make effective use of synonyms.

Understand how words are constructed

Learning objective
- understand the origin of some words and how they are put together.

Words are made up of building blocks. Consonants and vowels form syllables, which then make a root word; this can be altered by the use of prefixes and suffixes (letters added onto the start or end of a word), or by adding another root word.

Getting you thinking

The English language contains over a million words, and a lot of them originated centuries ago in other countries. Over the years, we have put different words together to form new words with new meanings.

Look at these words and how they break down into different building blocks:

autocorrect: (prefix) auto + (root word) correct

refill: (prefix) re + (root word) fill

disagreement: (prefix) dis + (root word) agree + (suffix) ment

photosensitive: (prefix) photo + (root word) sense + (suffix) itive

1 What other words can you think of that begin with the prefixes 'auto', 're', 'dis' and 'photo' (for example, automobile, remove, discomfort and photocopy)?

2 What other words can you think of that end with the suffixes 'ment' and 'itive' (for example, commencement and repetitive)?

How does it work?

By adding prefixes and suffixes to root words, you change their meanings. A lot of these words have their origins in the ancient languages of Greek and Latin. For example, 'dis' and 're' are Latin for 'not' and 'again', whilst 'auto' and 'photo' are Greek for 'oneself' and 'light'.

So with the word 'refill', the Latin prefix 're' has been added to the Old English word 'fill' to create a word that means 'to fill again'.

With 'photosensitive', the Greek word 'photo' has been added to the French word 'sensitive' (or 'sensitif') to create a compound that means 'sensitive to light'.

3 Think of six more prefixes and suffixes.

a) Using a dictionary, explain the meaning of each one and the languages that it originates from.

b) Come up with two or three words that can be combined with each of your prefixes and suffixes to create a new meaning.

Words can also be created by adding two root words together to form a *compound*. For example, you can add the Old English word 'light' to the Latin word 'bulb' to make 'lightbulb'.

4 Look at the list of words below.

any	arm	bed	body	day
every	eye	fore	guard	head
home	life	night	made	man
more	over	paper	rest	room
sight	some	spread	store	super
sun	thing	time	to	under
wear	weight	where	wide	with

a) How many compounds can you create from them?

b) Using your knowledge of each individual word's meaning, can you work out what each of your compounds would mean?

My dear wife
I hug you
With love
And friendship.

My cherished spouse,
I embrace you
With passion
And desire.

Some progress

I can form some words, using prefixes, suffixes and root words.

Good progress 》》

I can form a range of words using prefixes, suffixes and root words accurately.

Excellent progress 》》》

I can build up an ambitious range of words, considering how they affect the tone of my writing.

Apply your skills

Words can have the same meaning (these are called synonyms), but – depending on the origin of the word – a different tone. For example, the Old English word 'hungry' and the Latin word 'famished' mean the same thing, but 'hungry' suggests feeling a little peckish whilst 'famished' suggests you are desperate to eat.

5 Look at the two short love poems on the right. Write an explanation of how the different words in each one help to create a different tone.

Use precise vocabulary to make your ideas clearer

Learning objective

- choose vocabulary to make your meaning absolutely clear.

Whether you are writing to describe, persuade, inform or advise, you need to choose your vocabulary so that the reader understands precisely what you mean.

Getting you thinking

Look at these two drafts of an opening to a ghost story. In the second draft, the student has worked on the vocabulary to give a clearer sense of how creepy the house is.

> **A**
>
> Charles walked up the stairs. A cool breeze accompanied the winter sunlight that poured through the open windows. He began to get a bit scared. He looked around, wondering if anyone else was about. The house was shadowy and falling down.
>
> **B**
>
> The boy crept up the stairs, holding his breath nervously. The ice cold wind whipped through the shattered windows. Shards of glass reflected his terrified expression. He spun round in a panic, convinced he was being followed. Shadows seemed to slide across the crumbling, mouldering walls.

1 Has she succeeded in improving her work?

How does it work?

The second draft gives a much clearer image of the creepy house. Notice movements and feelings:

- the boy 'crept' rather than just 'walked' because he was 'terrified'
- he 'spun' rather than 'looked around'
- the shadows 'seemed to slide' as if they are alive!

Notice details:

- the windows are 'shattered', not simply 'open'
- the 'crumbling, mouldering walls' sound very sinister.

Read this opening to a detective story.

> It was raining and there was lightning. Sir Alec Williams lay dead in a pool of blood. Detective Inspector Lazenby looked around the room for clues. The drawing-room curtains were open and the wind was coming through the open window. Wet footprints led from the body to the door and a gun was on the floor.

2 Rewrite the opening using more precise vocabulary. Try to give the reader a clear idea of the setting and create a mysterious atmosphere. Think about which

- **nouns** or **verbs** you could change to create a more vivid picture

- **adjectives** and **adverbs** you could use to add detail to your writing.

Apply your skills

3 Work in a group of four. Using separate sheets of paper, each write the opening paragraph of a story. Decide who will write

- a science-fiction story

- a spy story

- a romance story

- a story of your own choice.

Everyone should spend five minutes starting their story, then pass it on for the next person in the group to continue. Do this four times until everyone has written part of each story. Remember to use vocabulary that fits the genre.

4 Read the stories aloud and then discuss the vocabulary used in each one. Were the choices made suitable for the genre?

Together, pick out examples of strong writing and decide on improvements for weaker spots. What new verb, noun, adjective and adverb choices could you make to improve the writing?

Glossary

nouns: things, people, places or ideas

verbs: doing or being words (I *am*, he *runs*)

adjectives: words that describe a noun (the *fat* cat)

adverbs: words that describe a verb (he runs *quickly*)

Top tip

Use a thesaurus to find alternative words, but also use a dictionary to check that the word matches your meaning.

Check your progress

Some progress

I can choose words to make my story easy to understand.

Good progress

I can use a range of vocabulary to make the ideas in my story clear.

Excellent progress

I can use an ambitious range of vocabulary to express my ideas with clarity and precision.

Choose vocabulary that is appropriate for your purpose

Learning objective
- match your choice of words to the purpose of your writing.

You need to be able to select words that fit the *purpose* of your writing.

Getting you thinking

A student has written a piece to argue the benefits of children using mobile phones at school. In the second draft, he has tried to choose vocabulary to strengthen his argument.

> **A**
>
> Children can use mobile phones to improve their education. With internet access they can do research, discuss tasks on message boards and download different things that link to their learning. In schools where mobile phones have been used well in classrooms during lesson time, students' grades have gone up.
>
> **B**
>
> Children can utilise mobile phones to massively improve their education. With constant internet access they can tackle in-depth research, discuss complex tasks on message boards and download apps, video clips and resources that link to their learning. In schools where mobile phones have been exploited as an educational tool, students' grades have risen dramatically.

1 With a partner, discuss how successful the changes made to the vocabulary are.

2 Which words and phrases make the argument in the second draft more convincing?

How does it work?

In the second draft, the vocabulary is more detailed, specific and **emotive**, which helps the student to make his argument more convincing.

Glossary

emotive: designed to produce an emotion in the reader

For example:

- everyday verbs (such as 'use') have been replaced with more specific verbs that match the writer's argument by suggesting making the most of something ('utilise', 'exploited')

- adverbs (such as 'dramatically', 'massively') have been added to make the argument more emotive and suggest the writer truly believes in what they are arguing

- adjectives have been added (such as 'in-depth' and 'complex') to convey how difficult school work can be

- subject-specific words (such as 'apps') have been used to give examples of the educational benefits of mobile phones.

Now you try it

3 Look at the speech on the right, also about mobile phones. Rewrite the speech, using specific, detailed and emotive words to make a stronger argument.

Some words and phrases that could be improved are in italic. Also try adding adverbs and extra phrases to intensify the argument.

Apply your skills

4 Plan and draft an advice sheet for young people about how to stay safe when using the internet. You could include sections on search filters, chat rooms and online bullying.

The *idea* that we ban mobile phones at school is *silly*. It would be *bad* to *get rid of* something *very* useful. Mobiles are an *important part* of our lives: keeping us in contact with our *friends and family*, as well as *keeping us safe*. My mum *worries* and *likes me to* contact her if I'm going to be late home.

Checklist for success

✔ Use subject-related vocabulary and specific words to clarify your advice.

✔ Select words carefully so that you sound as if you are suggesting, rather than ordering your reader to do something (for example, 'You could...', 'Have you thought about...')

✔ Make your advice sound friendly and sensible (for example, 'Chat rooms can be brilliant, but you're still talking to a stranger so it makes sense not to share anything that's private...')

✔ Use connectives that show sequence – 'firstly', 'secondly', 'next', 'finally').

Check your progress

Some progress

I can choose words to get across some different ideas.

Good progress

I can use a range of vocabulary that matches my purpose.

Excellent progress

I can use an ambitious range of vocabulary to create specific effects.

Make effective use of synonyms

Learning objective

- vary your vocabulary to make your writing more interesting.

Words that have similar meanings are called synonyms. Using synonyms will stop your writing getting repetitive.

Getting you thinking

Read this extract from the novel *A Handful of Dust*.

> Outside, it was soft English weather; mist in the hollows and pale sunshine on the hills; the **coverts** had ceased dripping, for there were no leaves to hold the recent rain, but the undergrowth was wet, dark in the shadows, **iridescent** where the sun caught it; the lanes were soggy and there was water running in the ditches.
>
> *A Handful of Dust* by Evelyn Waugh

1 With a partner, pick out all the different words associated with *wet* and *light* that are used to create an engaging description of the English countryside.

Glossary

coverts: thickets or woodland

iridescent: shimmering, multicoloured

How does it work?

Waugh uses words like 'mist', 'dripping', 'rain' and 'soggy' to build up an image of the continually wet countryside.

To convey the type of light, Waugh uses 'soft, pale sunshine' and 'iridescent': it's not the blazing hot sun of summer but a cooler, springtime sun that makes everything glitter.

Not all these words are *synonyms* of wet and light, but they all help to build up a vivid picture.

Top tip

Try never to use the same word twice in a paragraph – always ask yourself: 'is there a more interesting way I could say that?' or 'how could I put that differently?'

Now you try it

2 With a partner, make a list of other synonyms you could use for 'wet' and 'light'.

3 Take it in turns to suggest synonyms for each of the words below. If you get stuck, check in a thesaurus.

nice	dark	ugly
weak	take	small
run	make	large

4 You can use synonyms in all types of writing, not just describing. Using a thesaurus, find synonyms for the word 'important' to complete this persuasive speech.

> I am here to talk about the _____ issue of the environment. It is _____ that we stop polluting the atmosphere and realise how _____ caring for our world really is. A particularly _____ factor in reducing pollution is recycling. We play a _____ role in teaching our children about cutting down waste.

Top tip

Choose synonyms with the exact meaning you want for your writing. Whether you are using a thesaurus or picking words from memory, you should check your choices in a dictionary.

Apply your skills

5 Imagine you are on holiday. Write a postcard to your partner: one of you should be having a holiday filled with sun and heat; the other should be having non-stop rain and freezing temperatures.

Use synonyms to describe to each other how your holiday is going.

6 Now try using synonyms in some informative writing

Complete a report for the police concerning an argument between two neighbours about noise. The catch is that you *cannot* use the words 'said', 'loud' or 'quiet'. Find as many suitable synonyms as you can.

Check your progress

Some progress

I can use some synonyms to make my report more varied.

Good progress

I can use a range of synonyms to keep my report varied and interesting.

Excellent progress

I can use an ambitious range of synonyms that are effective and varied.

Check your progress

Some progress

- [ ] I can use some prefixes and suffixes accurately.
- [ ] I can use words to make my work easy to understand.
- [ ] I can use some words to get different ideas across.
- [ ] I can use some synonyms to make my work more varied.

Good progress

- [ ] I can use a range of prefixes and suffixes accurately.
- [ ] I can use a range of vocabulary to make my ideas clear.
- [ ] I can use a range of vocabulary that matches my purpose.
- [ ] I can use a range of synonyms to keep my work varied and interesting.

Excellent progress

- [ ] I can use prefixes and suffixes in order to build up an ambitious range of words in my writing.
- [ ] I can use an ambitious range of vocabulary to bring clarity and precision to my writing.
- [ ] I can use an ambitious range of vocabulary to create various effects that will meet the purpose of my writing.
- [ ] I can use an ambitious range of effective synonyms that are engaging and help to make my work stand out.

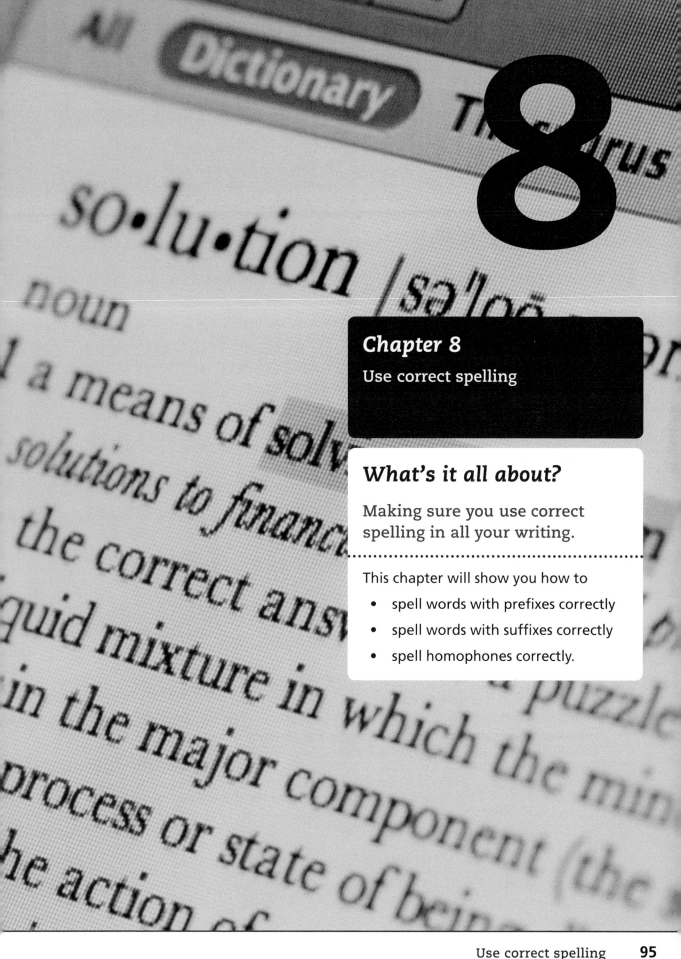

Chapter 8

Use correct spelling

What's it all about?

Making sure you use correct spelling in all your writing.

This chapter will show you how to

- spell words with prefixes correctly
- spell words with suffixes correctly
- spell homophones correctly.

Spell words with prefixes correctly

Learning objective

- be accurate in your spelling of words with a prefix.

Prefixes are groups of letters that are added to the start of a word to change its meaning.

Getting you thinking

1 How many words can you think of that begin with the prefix un- (for example, 'undo')?

How does it work?

Prefixes are added to the *beginning* of words to make a new word – for example, 'submarine'.

Most of the time, they can simply be added to the start of a word, but some prefixes are bit more difficult and come with a spelling rule.

When a prefix ends in -e and the word begins with e, or with the prefix non-, you should include a hyphen after the prefix: re-enter, non-fiction.

Another prefix is in- or im-, which means 'not': informal, imbalanced. You should always use in-, unless the word you are adding it to begins with a letter b, m or p, in which case you use im-.

Now you try it

2 Copy down these prefixes. For each one, come up with a different example from the one in the box. An explanation of each prefix if given to help you.

Prefix	Explanation	Example 1	Example 2
dis	to show a negative or remove	disadvantage	dismiss
de	remove	deodorise	
fore	in advance	forethought	
mis	wrongly	misprint	

Prefix	Explanation	Example 1	Example 2
non	not	non-stop	
over	above, outer, or too much	overconfident	
pre	before	precooked	
re	again	resubmit	
sub	under	submarine	
un	(reversal of a word's meaning)	unhelpful	

3 Add the following prefixes to the given words. Remember when you need to use a hyphen. Write down their new meanings afterwards (you might need to use a dictionary).

a) de- activate, energise, escalate, face, frost, press, rail

b) pre- cook, establish, exist, historic, pay, school, view

c) re- charge, cover, elect, enact, enter, fuel, try

4 Add the correct in- or im- prefix to the following words. Again, write down their new meaning afterwards.

correct	edible	fallible	mature	mobile
patient	perfect	polite	sincere	visible

Apply your skills

There are always exceptions to rules. For example, according to the rules on these pages, you should write 'prerecord' but actually it takes a hyphen: 'pre-record'. But don't worry – there aren't many exceptions and, after a while, you'll learn which spellings break the rules.

5 With a partner, play a spelling game. Using a dictionary, find words with prefixes and challenge each other to spell them correctly. You get one point each time you use the prefix correctly and two points if you spell the whole word correctly.

Use the rules you have learned to help you. As you play, you may come across some of the exceptions mentioned above, so the dictionary's answer is final!

Check your progress

Some progress

I can spell words that use the most common prefixes correctly.

Good progress

I can spell most words that use prefixes correctly.

Excellent progress

I can spell words that use prefixes correctly.

Spell words with suffixes correctly

Learning objective

• be accurate in spelling words with a suffix.

Suffixes are groups of letters that are added to the end of a word to change its meaning.

Getting you thinking

1 How many different suffixes can you come up with to alter the meaning of the word 'sleep'? For example: 'over' = 'sleepover'.

How does it work?

Suffixes are placed at the *end* of words. The most commonly used suffix is '-ing'. Although there are some exceptions, here are some general rules:

If the word ends in an -e, simply replace the -e with -ing:

take becomes taking.

If a word contains a long vowel sound (the ah sound in arm, the ee in sea, the aw in pour, the er in purse, the oo in group) before the final consonant, just add -ing:

calming, feeling, clawing, hurting, shooting.

If a word contains a short vowel sound (the a sound in cat, the i in sit, the o in hot, the u in sun) before the final consonant, double the last consonant and then add -ing:

trapping, swimming, robbing, cutting.

Now you try it

2 Add the -ing suffix correctly to the words in the table below.

alarm	brake	burn	farm	feel
gnaw	hit	learn	peel	pop
recruit	rip	rot	run	sag
snore	stun	tag	wait	whip

> **Top tip**
>
> Think of the two words 'hope' and 'hop'. In 'hope' the vowel is long 'oh' and in 'hop' it is short. 'Hope' becomes 'hoping' and 'hop' becomes 'hopping'.

One exception to these rules is with the short vowel sound e (as in bed or help).

3 Using a dictionary, check how the spelling changes when you add -ing to the following words:

dread	forget	head	interest	let
relent	set	shed	tread	wed

Apply your skills

You can use a suffix to turn lots of adjectives into adverbs – just add -ly (for example, 'slow' becomes 'slowly').

4 Working with a partner, see how many adjectives you can turn into adverbs in five minutes. Afterwards, if there are any that you're unsure of, ask your teacher or check them in a dictionary.

Suffixes can also turn adjectives into nouns, and nouns into adjectives. For example, 'sad' can become 'sadness', 'home' can become 'homeless'.

5 Using a dictionary, see how many adjectives you can turn into nouns just by using the suffix -ness, and then see how many nouns you can turn into adjectives simply by adding -less.

You can also turn nouns into adjectives by adding -ful. For example, 'hope' can become 'hopeful', or 'beauty' can become 'beautiful'. With words that end in -y, it gets changed to -i before you add -ful.

In addition, suffixes can turn verbs into nouns, and nouns into verbs. For example, 'govern' can become 'government', or 'person' become 'personify'.

6 See how many verbs you can turn into nouns by adding -ment. Then try changing some nouns into verbs using either -ise, or -ify.

If the noun ends in an e or a y, you'll have to remove it before adding your suffix.

> **Top tip**
>
> Watch out for adjectives ending in a 'y'. If they do, take off the 'y' and add '-ily' ('naughty' becomes 'naughtily').

Check your progress

Some progress >>

I can spell words that use the most common suffixes correctly.

Good progress >>

I can spell most words that use suffixes correctly.

Excellent progress >>>

I can spell words that use suffixes correctly.

Spell homophones correctly

Learning objective

- choose the correct spelling for words that sound the same.

Homophones are words that sound the same but have different meanings and spellings. It is important that you learn to tell the difference between them so that your writing always makes sense.

How does it work?

there / their / they're

These are homophones that often cause spelling problems. Here are the different meanings:

- *there* = place or position ('We parked the car over *there*.')

- *their* = ownership ('It was *their* car.')

- *they're* = abbreviation of 'they are' ('*They're* getting out of the car.')

Now you try it

1 Copy out this paragraph, correcting the homophones in red.

> I was walking along the street when their was a loud noise. Two boys came running from they're house, there faces full of panic. I asked if they're was anything I could do to help but they just pointed back at there hallway and shouted, 'There still in their!'

How does it work?

its / it's and **your / you're**

These pairs of homophones are often confused. Here are the different meanings:

- *its* = ownership, just like his/her ('The bird had hurt *its* wing.')

- *it's* = abbreviation of 'it is' ('*It's* cold outside.')

- *your* = ownership ('Where is *your* coat?')

- *you're* = abbreviation of 'you are' ('*You're* going to school.')

Now you try it

2 Look at these pairs of homophones. Using a dictionary, check the different meanings of both words in each pair. Write a sentence using each pair of words.

hear / here	no / know	one / won
sea / see	to / too / two	wear / where

Apply your skills

3 Rewrite the paragraph below, filling in the blanks with the correct homophones from the list above.

She liked _____ stand by the _____ and _____ the sound of the waves. If it was _____ cold, she would _____ a fur coat she had once _____ at cards. _____ or _____ people would _____ her and acknowledge her curiously: _____ one seemed to _____ her, or _____ she lived.

4 Now proofread the paragraph below and change any of the homophones that have been used incorrectly.

I couldn't bare to see him – couldn't even stand the site of him. He'd been so shore of himself; thinking that he was sum kind of hero, but I new the truth. Their had just been the too of us there hanging around in the newsagent. I was looking for some suites to by, but I didn't realise that he was busy steeling stationary. It was only when wee started to leave that the shop-owner shouted, 'Weight! Your not going too leave without buying those things are you?' I turned and staired at him. Then I turned on my tale and ran.

Top tip

With these words, always ask yourself: 'Is there a letter missing? What does this word really mean?'

Check your progress

Some progress

I can spell most common words but sometimes confuse words that sound the same.

Good progress

I can spell common words and most homophones correctly.

Excellent progress

I can spell most words, including complex vocabulary.

Check your progress

Some progress

- [ ] I can spell most common words but confuse words that sound the same.
- [ ] I can spell plurals but have some trouble with other word endings.
- [ ] I can spot some homophones.

Good progress

- [ ] I can spell common words and most homophones correctly.
- [ ] I can use prefixes correctly and use suffixes to spell the endings of most words correctly.
- [ ] I can spell some common homophones correctly.

Excellent progress

- [ ] I can spell most words, including complex vocabulary.
- [ ] I can use suffixes to spell the endings of complex words correctly.
- [ ] I can spell a variety of homophones confidently.

Teacher Guide

The general aim of these books is the practical and everyday application of **Assessment for Learning**: to ensure every child knows how they are doing and what they need to do to improve. The specific aim is to help every child progress and for you to be able to track that progress.

The books empower the student by modelling the essential skills needed, and by allowing them to practise and then demonstrate independently what they know and can do across every reading and writing strand. They help the teacher by providing opportunities to gather and review secure evidence of day-to-day progress in each strand. Where appropriate (and especially at lower levels) the books facilitate teacher scaffolding of such learning and assessment.

The series offers exercises and examples that we hope will not only help students add descriptive power and nuance to their vocabulary but also expand the grammatical constructions they can access and use: above all, the ability to write and read in sentences (paragraphs, texts) – to think consciously in complete thoughts. We aim at fuller, more complex self-expression – developing students' ability to express themselves simply or with complexity and the sense to choose when each mode of expression is apt.

Each chapter progresses through a series of emphases, to be practised and mastered before bringing it back to the real reading and writing (of whole texts) in which all these – suitably polished – skills can be applied.

The *Aiming for…* series has been extremely popular in schools. This new edition retains all that was successful about the old but has improved it further in several significant ways.

- This book positively tracks progress in the new curriculum, so each chapter has been updated to ensure thorough coverage of the Key Stage 3 Programme of Study and the Grammar, Vocabulary and Punctuation Appendix to the Key Stage 2 Programme of Study.

- The new progress categories of Some/Good/Excellent correspond to the old sublevels of low Level 5, secure Level 5 and high Level 5.

- A matching chart to the new curriculum is available on www.collins.co.uk/aimingfor.

- The 'Applying your skills' section of each topic is now consistently focused on longer writing tasks designed to build the writing stamina and independence needed for GCSE.

Gareth Calway and Mike Gould
Series Editors

1 Capture your reader's interest and imagination

The Collins publications *Bound For Jamaica* (Read On series) and Olaudah Equiano *From Slavery to Freedom* (Big Cat series) are packed with reliable, student-friendly information and imaginative reconstruction of the subject covered in this lesson.

Getting you thinking
Read the extract aloud to the class, helping them with any unfamiliar vocabulary.

You may want to contextualise the passage by sharing some of the key facts about slavery and the slave trade:

www.understandingslavery.com/ teachingslavetrade/introduction/keyfacts/ www.primarycolours.net

Now you try it
Students are initially aiming to write around 200 words at most. The key point here is for them to imagine what the experience would be like, and to put themselves in the mind of a child who has been separated from his or her family and taken off into a terrifying, completely unfamiliar environment. The ship would be the climax of a long series of such misfortunes.

Students could start by jotting down one idea or image for each of the senses, then develop these notes into an account of 200 words or so describing their experiences.

Apply your skills
Some useful websites to direct students towards might be

http://www.understandingslavery.com/ teachingslavetrade/
http://www.bbc.co.uk/history/british/ abolition/
http://www.guardian.co.uk/ uk/interactive/2008/oct/13/ black-history-month-timeline

2 Write in a form that fits your purpose

Getting you thinking
Get students to talk about the effect of repetition/contrasts, the consonance of 'smack/cat/deck', verbs such as 'cramm'd' and 'stow'd', etc.

Once they have discussed the alternative types of writing in Activity 2, ask a few pairs to feed back to the rest of the class. Draw out the type of language these forms might use. For example, a letter to a newspaper or a Facebook post might be written in emotional language; a leaflet or website to support the campaign would be factual; a speech to Parliament might acknowledge both sides of the argument.

Remind students that although we now regard slavery as immoral, the arguments in favour of it were seriously made in the 1790s by those who profited from slavery. (40% of Bristol's population depended on the trade, but even then Bristolians like Hannah More argued against it and no one would argue for it today.)

How does it work?
Show the students examples of the different kinds of writing and have a class discussion. How does each make them feel? What kind of words do they use? How does the tone of each differ?

Now you try it
Read through the poem 'The Sorrows of Yamba' with the class again, and check

their understanding. If necessary, help them identify the emotive words in the poem that should be omitted in their courtroom account in order to present the facts in a more formal way.

Apply your skills
The websites and books suggested for Topic 1 will also be useful here. At the end of the lesson, draw together the learning by discussing the differences between accounts in the first (Activity 3) and third person (Activity 4), based on their different forms.

3 Plan, develop and shape your writing

Getting you thinking
Read through the extract with students. Explain that they need to pick out the most important information first: where the accident occurred, what has happened, who is involved, whether an ambulance should be called. It might help students to know that this situation comes from a play set in an urban wasteland, based on a real incident in which a joyrider died.

How does it work?
Share these examples with students, to help explain the different approaches.

The following call was recorded at the time:

Hello, yes – oh my God – I need an ambulance now…yes, on the road up to the Corbenic Estate – it needs to be where all this accident and stuff is happening… where the roads go round and there are five different roads going off in every direction…

The event was reported in writing like this:

An ambulance was called to the RTA/ possible crime scene at the Fiveways roundabout on Corbenic Way.

Now you try it
Encourage students to add as much detail and information as they can, as they extend their plan.

Apply your skills
An extension activity for students who finish early or for more able students:

- How would this accident be reported in a local newspaper?

- What different details might be included?

- How would the way the report is organised be different?

Get them to discuss these ideas with a partner, then plan and draft a front-page newspaper report about the accident.

Remind students that newspaper articles have to get to the point quickly. Their first paragraph must include the facts (Who? What? Where? Why? When?) before they go on to discuss the story.

4 Write powerfully, vividly and precisely

Getting you thinking
This lesson encourages students to make imaginative – yet concise – word pictures by first asking them to draw actual pictures in response to some poetic images.

How does it work?
Draw out with students that the two poetic descriptions concentrate on the image. They cut out filler phrases like 'There was…', 'I looked up above…', 'which was…'

Help students to see that

- the first poem uses a *simile* to compare the autumn moon to a red-faced farmer. The picture of the moon leaning towards you as it appears over a hedge is clear, precise and strong.

- the second poem uses an *extended metaphor* to compare the sea crashing over the shore with a forest blowing in the wind, or to compare a fir tree blowing in a wind to the sea's waves.

Explain to students that choosing striking words and images and cutting out 'filler' phrases will help them create powerful writing. They want their reader to absorb every word and not 'skim read' because they are bored!

Now you try it
Make it clear to students that the person they have strong feelings about can't be anyone in the room and that they must keep the person's identity secret.

Other ideas to get them to generate images include: a city, a month, a colour, an animal, a vehicle, a kitchen utensil, an article of clothing.

5 Write clearly and analytically

Getting you thinking
In case students don't know, explain that a 'Chelsea tractor' is a 4x4 or any vehicle perceived as being too big for local roads. Draw out the informal, slightly indignant tone of the first statement, compared to the more measured tone of the second.

How does it work?
Remind students that even a thoughtful point of view can sound biased if expressed informally or colloquially ('I reckon'), so writing formally is a way of showing how considered their opinion is. People will listen more readily. Modals ('It could be argued that…') will make their point of view sound more thoughtful and convincing.

Now you try it
The facts and figures speak for themselves. If 9% of Norfolk people work in tourism, it is clearly an important industry. But facts and figures can be argued about. Tourism brings much more work to Norfolk than farming does, so some might say that the farmer is wrong to protest and put off the tourists. However, tourists have bought local people's homes as holiday homes and changed much of the rural county into a seasonal destination instead of a 'real' one.

At this stage, students are only practising language that *sounds* reasonable, not stating whether or not they agree with one side or another.

Apply your skills
Help students use reasoned discussion to express their beliefs. They could be encouraged to find out a bit more about the effects of tourism in rural areas before writing up their thoughts. They might consider the point that if farmers didn't attractively manage the land, woods, crops etc. then tourists might not visit anyway.

6 Develop a clear and convincing voice

Getting you thinking
Read the extract aloud and discuss the questions as a class. Also ask them:

- Why do they think Kevin Brooks chose to write in the first person?

- How does this help us get a picture of Martyn's thoughts and feelings?

How does it work?

You can help make sure students understand the effects of careful word choice in the first person by looking at the short sentences Martyn uses to complain about Alex's lateness ('I'm never late for anything...'). Draw out with students that he comes across as very precise (choosing his words carefully) and well organised – someone who likes to have everything just so.

Now you try it

Encourage students to spend time creating and developing the character of Alex before they start planning. They should pick up all the clues they can find in the extract first. Explain that careful thought and planning now will make their writing much easier and more effective later.

Chapter 2 Produce texts that are appropriate to task, reader and purpose

1 Choose the right tone for persuasive texts

Getting you thinking

Read the letter with the class. If they were Benedict Cumberbatch, would they want to come and help? Ask students to suggest what the purpose is (to persuade) and discuss the tone – is it very serious and impersonal, or is too familiar and friendly? Or does it get the approach about right?

How does it work?

Take students through the explanation of some of the techniques used.

- Can they find examples to illustrate how the letter is formal but friendly?

- Can they find any other positive adjectives?

- Can they identify the rhetorical question in the last paragraph?

Now you try it

Students could work in pairs to jointly compose their version of the letter to Mo Farah. Start by identifying what is *wrong* with the letter. Draw out that the tone is too informal ('Hiya', 'mates'). It is too blunt (short sentences with little detail about the charity or the fete). The focus is not sustained (he refers to Usain Bolt).

Apply your skills

Scaffold on the board how the letter might look. For example:

Formal welcome ('Dear...')

Paragraph 1: what you admire about X

Paragraph 2: why you are writing – what the 'problem' is

Paragraph 3: how X can help.

2 Improve characterisation in narrative and descriptive writing

Getting you thinking

Ask students to suggest questions raised by the opening and write them on the board. For example, 'Why is Matt at the station?'; 'What mistake is he about to make?'; 'Why is he wearing tatty clothes?' etc.

How does it work?

For each of these details, ask students to suggest examples: a verb and an adverb to suggest a character's actions ('standing sadly by the door'), and write these on the board. In particular, make sure they are clear about 'showing' rather than 'telling' (for example, we are shown that Matt is perhaps poor/ hasn't much money through the clothes he wears).

Now you try it
Read the whole extract with the class, then read it through again a section at a time. Students could put up their hands as they come across a listed writing technique. Encourage them to look for additional techniques. For example, what do they notice about the length of the paragraphs? What is the effect? Then ask them about their overall impression of Matt.

Elicit the idea that by the end we can see that he is quite magnetic due to his apperance and hints at danger, but he also invites our sympathies due to his 'problems'.

Students should work on their own for their paragraph about Dina. Then hear some examples and ask them to evaluate whether the three elements have been covered.

Apply your skills
Students should aim to write about 200 words here. The image is there as a stimulus but some students may prefer to develop a character of their own. They should be thinking about who the character is, what they do, their personality traits and where they have been or where they are going.

Remind students that good writers will reveal a character's personality through his or her actions, as shown in the extracts.

3 Use factual information effectively when writing to argue

First, make sure that students understand fully what is meant by a writer's viewpoint. Ask them to think of as many examples as they can of types of writing where it is important to develop a viewpoint. Explain that expressing a clear viewpoint makes writing much more lively and interesting.

Getting you thinking
Ask pairs to read the script aloud, and then discuss the questions. Take feedback and draw out the idea that both speakers object to the mistreatment of exotic pets, but that they disagree over the solutions. The activist does offer a reason – 'loads of people…set them free' but it is an *assertion* that lacks factual evidence.

How does it work?
Go back over the expert's words: can students identify at least one more example of each of the techniques listed? (formal language: 'non-native species'; adverbs: 'only', 'definitely'; facts: '30 per cent accidental')

Now you try it
Read the article together as a class.

- Discuss what the viewpoint is.

- Is any evidence provided, or are the ideas assertions?

- Is the language professional-sounding? Why/why not?

Model the beginning of the article using some of the techniques suggested. For example:

'Many might argue that as a nation we do not care for our domestic animals. However, I believe strongly that…'

Apply your skills
You might need to provide a menu of words and phrases for students to use in their alternative version. For example:

only, yet, despite this, however, even though, a small/large number…, a low/ high proportion…, nearly/just over…

4 Use the active and passive for different effects in non-fiction writing

Getting you thinking

Students can discuss the two headlines in pairs and then feed back their responses. The first uses the more informal and personal 'Jess' (readers would know who she was) and places her at the start of the sentence so the emphasis is on *her* victory. The second foregrounds the 'world record', suggesting the event itself is more important than the person.

How does it work?

Make sure that everyone is clear about the two forms.

It is worth pointing out that not *all* active sentences can be turned into passive ones. Generally, *transitive verbs* (those that take a direct object) can:

'I [s] won [v] the race [direct object]'

'The race was won by me [passive].'

Intransitive verbs (which do not have direct objects) cannot usually be turned into passive forms:

'I [s] waited [v] at the start-line' (prepositional phrase) cannot become *'The start-line was waited at by me'*!

Now you try it

Read the memo aloud. Then ask the students to work quickly in pairs to highlight the passive forms. These could be: 'Why sports day was cancelled'; 'Chairs had been put out'; 'parents welcomed'; 'it was noticed'; 'Shelter was offered'.

Take feedback on why the passive voice is used – in this case because the teacher wants to escape responsibility by not mentioning that he was the one who cancelled the event.

However, point out that the passive is also often used when a more objective tone is needed – for example, when reporting the facts of an event. Ask students to complete the rewriting of the rest of the memo on their own.

Apply your skills

It is relatively easy to change each of these sets of notes into a passive form ('At 5pm the city was surrounded by rebel soldiers'), but students need to build a full report so they should add further details. They can do this by adding adjectives or adjectival phrases to nouns ('…rebel soldiers, *armed to the hilt with heavy weaponry*') and by linking parts of the report with adverbials of time ('By the following day…').

5 Write in an appropriate style for your purpose

How does it work?

Explain to students that the first example is an encyclopedia entry. Most students should be familiar with websites like Wikipedia. The text presents a series of factual statements about Brighton, written in a neutral way to *inform* the reader. Ask students why they think it might be important for encyclopedia-type texts to be neutral in this way.

The second extract comes from a newspaper article persuading readers that Brighton is worth visiting. It presents similar information but in a very different way. For example, the writer uses

- adverbs and adjectives such as 'surprisingly good'
- verbs and adverbs such as 'roam freely', to make visiting Brighton seem appealing

- vivid details to make the city come to life ('skateboarding Jack Russell')
- direct address such as 'you' and imperative verbs such as 'Head to…'.

Now you try it
Students could compose their text in pairs, and then peer evaluate what they have done, measuring its success against the second text about Brighton. Remind them that for these purposes they should keep the text in the present tense if they can.

Apply your skills
Explain to students that they should write this text as more of a narrative account, but one that still creates a positive picture of Brighton. Ask them to suggest how a narrative account may differ slightly from a more general persuasive text. It would

- have a logical time-order (the day's events and impressions)
- be written in the past tense ('I arrived in Brighton just as…')
- use some of the techniques of good descriptive writing (vivid imagery, specific nouns, etc.)
- probably *not* refer to the reader.

Chapter 3 Organise and present whole texts effectively, sequencing and structuring information, ideas and events

1 Structure your writing clearly

This lesson focuses on a story told in a comic-strip format – the lack of words means that the writer has to structure the story clearly (in frames) so that the reader can easily follow what is happening. Ask students to bring in a range of different comic-strip stories to compare.

Getting you thinking
Spend some time asking a number of students to read their descriptions of the events in the comic strip, so that they can see how the sequence of events is clear – even if the words and style are different. They could compare their ideas in pairs. What similarities and differences are there in how they have interpreted the story?

How does it work?
Talk through some various structures for different types of writing. Reiterate that the best structure to choose depends on the *purpose* of the writing.

Apply your skills
Explain to students that they should start by planning a simple storyline, then divide it up into a series of frames that will make the key events clear. Stress that artistic style is not important – stick figures would be fine.

As an extension to this activity, students could write up both sides of the whole 'argument', first giving their own side and then the other. The structure for this is neither time-narrative nor informing point by point. It is a *three-part structure*. Guide them in planning as follows:

- Arrange into three paragraphs how you felt when waiting.

- Add three paragraphs giving the excuses. (For example, 'Sue said she couldn't contact me because…')

- Add a conclusion in which you argue for who deserves the most sympathy. This should take into account all the points but not repeat them in detail.

2 Build your ideas across a piece of writing

How does it work
As well as the repeated comparisons of heat with extreme experiences, point out the repeated contrasts of the words used to describe the heat with words describing more pleasant things ('air conditioning', 'waffles'). Other cohesive devices within sentences are the relative clauses ('As I stepped out of the porch...', 'my feet sticking to the road').

Apply your skills
Remind students to *link* their sentences so that the piece develops and shows how their ideas are building. For example:

First of all... Later that day...
It was nearly midday when...
At the end... Firstly...
Secondly... Some time had passed when...
It was only a matter of time before...

3 Organise and present a text for audience and purpose

Getting you thinking
Remind students of the importance of presentation as part of the range of techniques that can be used to achieve their purpose in writing. Presentation can be used to draw the reader in as well as to get the key message across as clearly as possible.

Different devices and features are used for different types of text. A rock concert, for example, might use appealing pictures and bright colours, but in a campaign against drink driving, colours might be more sombre.

How does it work?
Feed back students' ideas about who the Animal Aid leaflet is aimed at. They have probably realised that it is aimed at young adults. We can tell this from the design (the fonts look edgy and modern, designed to appeal to a young audience), the colours, pictures and headings (which reveal the leaflet's purpose of persuading the reader to join Animal Aid).

They may also have worked out the intended audience from the language and content of the leaflet.

Now you try it
Briefly discuss with students what sort of key changes would need to be made for the leaflet to appeal to – and be suitable for – a much younger age range.

Apply your skills
Remind students to keep the leaflet they design appropriate, and not to cause offence. It can still have a relaxed and informal style.

4 Summarise and adapt information clearly

Getting you thinking
Students should note the following tips: 5 a day is vital; contains fibre, vitamins and minerals; protects against 'heart disease and some cancers'; doesn't have to be expensive; may include canned and frozen food.

Apply your skills
Remind students to think about headings, bullets, imperatives, direct address etc. as well as about how images/colours could support the text (for example, multicoloured type for the heading to reflect different coloured fruit and veg).

5 Organise narrative writing effectively

How does it work?
Go through the five-part structure, explaining to students what each stage entails. Ask students to discuss in pairs a film they have seen recently, or a book they have just read. Does its plot fit the five-part story structure? Discussing the structure of their film or book should help students to see that, however complex a narrative might initially seem, it can usually be stripped down to this structure.

Point out that the rising action/climax/falling action part of a story is where the main action takes place. This is often a conflict or problem (a mystery to be solved or a challenge for a character to overcome). Something crucial happens that will affect the rest of the story. There can be several conflicts in a novel.

Apply your skills
Remind students to spend some time planning the five sections of their story before they begin writing the climax.

After they have written the climax to their story, get them to swap with a partner, who should try to guess some of the events in other parts (what had happened to lead up to the climax? How might the story end?)

As an extension activity, allow students to write up their whole story based on their five-part plan.

6 Make your ending link back to your opening

Getting you thinking
Once pairs have read through and discussed the article, ask for feedback and discuss with the class how the article is structured. What important points are included? Go through it paragraph by paragraph.

How does it work?
Go through these points in relation to the article. Ask students what they think is the purpose of the piece as established in the opening (to inform about the working life of Victorian children). In what ways does the final paragraph remind them of this?

Now you try it
It might be helpful for students to start by drawing up a list of the 'bad' things about being a child now. They could focus on school-related issues (uniform policy, canteen food, school toilets) or wider issues.

Chapter 4   Construct paragraphs and use cohesion within and between paragraphs

1 Use paragraphs in fiction

Getting you thinking
Read the extract to the class. What effect does each part have on the students?

How does it work?
Which of the reasons can students spot in the extract from *Thursday's Child*?

Now you try it
This offers students the opportunity to do a similar activity with a later extract from the same novel.

The original layout of the passage is as follows:

From my place lying on the floor before the fire, I did not need to look up to know Da's eyes had darted to me.

'It was Tin, Mam,' I said listlessly.

'Ah!' Da exclaimed, and his hand slapped the table.

'What do you mean, it was Tin?'

'Harper, enough!'

I crooked my neck to peer at him. 'We have to tell, Da. People are asking.'

Apply your skills
Encourage students to try out all the different reasons for starting a new paragraph in their story.

2 Use cohesive devices to link ideas within and between paragraphs

Getting you thinking
Students might like to know that in the original source, the narrator of this dramatic monologue is Oliver Cromwell's own severed head!

How does it work?
Other linking devices used include

- **synonyms:** for example, 'axe(man)' and 'blade'
- **ellipsis:** '(he had) not a hair out of place'.

Now you try it
The four-year-old boy Oliver Cromwell really did meet King James VI of Scotland on his way to becoming King James I of England (Charles I's father), at his rich uncle's house in 1603. Baby Oliver was said to have been taken up to the roof of this house by a monkey, as described.

The three time frames and their respective stories – Oliver as a baby, Oliver dreaming about meeting the king and Oliver as a four-year-old meeting the king – are a natural way of dividing into paragraphs, rather than by place (which is the same throughout). The place being the same adds further cohesion to the story. The first paragraph of their story need not be the first in time.

Apply your skills
If it suits their purpose, students could use a flashback, with cohesive devices of time such as 'Years before…' Or they could use another order with devices such as 'When he *did* meet the king, he was…'.

3 Use paragraphs in argument texts

Getting you thinking
This section looks at the use of paragraphs in an argument text, which can be more complex. Students need to be clear that such a text will often refer to both sides of the argument and that there is a choice to be made between going through all the arguments on one side first, then the other, or alternating between the two. They will probably find it easier to adopt the former approach but they should be aware of the latter.

How does it work?
Help students to relate the four points to the extract. Do they think it is effective as an argumentative piece?

- The first paragraph tells the reader what the essay will be about.
- The second paragraph develops the first by stating: 'An argument for this idea is…'.

- The third paragraph changes viewpoint by setting out the arguments against the proposal. It links to the second by using the connective 'However…'.

- The fourth paragraph uses another connective, 'Equally', to refer back to the previous argument and to introduce the writer's own concluding viewpoint.

Now you try it
The proposal that students are arguing about – that the driving age should be lowered to 14 – is likely to appeal, but they could undertake the same activity with regard to any proposal that interests them.

4 Sequence paragraphs to give information effectively

Getting you thinking
If necessary, explain what a flow chart is by modelling one on the board.

How does it work?
Go over each paragraph, taking suggestions from the class.

- The text starts with a paragraph explaining why it is a good idea to have a qualified instructor.

- The next paragraph gives more reasons for having proper lessons.

- The next talks about fear and how to overcome it by having a proper instructor.

- The next describes finding your lead foot.

- The final paragraph encourages the reader to book a lesson.

Now you try it
Students might notice that the penultimate paragraph adds an entertaining aside as a link through to the final paragraph and the rest of the article. Some might say this is the wrong place to bring in a 'new' subject; others that it extends interest. What do students think? The shortness of the final paragraph is an effective 'call to action'.

Apply your skills
How students order and arrange their text will depend on the exact purpose of their advice sheet. Ask students to consider:

- Is it to help someone learn how to do something? (Perhaps the advice sheet could be organised as a series of instructions.)

- Is it to persuade someone to try a new sport? (The advice sheet would need a persuasive, appealing opening paragraph and a concluding paragraph that returns to this point.)

5 Organise poems using stanzas

Getting you thinking
Explain to students that stanzas are not the same as verses. Traditional poems were made up of stanzas and refrains/choruses. The 'verse' is actually a stanza plus the refrain or chorus. Stanzas, like paragraphs, are often used to introduce a new topic, image, event or theme.

In some poems the shape and length of stanzas will be predetermined by the form, so there the poet's content is creatively shaped by the form. Examples are the ballad, the villanelle (as here) and the ode.

It is worth pointing out the enjambment in this poem (such as between the third and fourth stanzas). Ask students how it contributes to the effect of the poem.

How does it work?

Highlight to students that the stanzas are linked by the repetition of alternate key lines repeated from the first stanza. A single rhyme also links every second line.

The last stanza is a (fatal) 'conclusion' to the rest. It has an extra line, sums up all that's gone before and refers back to the start by repeating both key lines. It is where the poem – and the boy – was always going.

Explain that some poems might not tell a story, but describe a place or an emotion instead. These poems might change stanza to show a change of place, time or viewpoint in a similar way to how paragraphs are used in stories, in information-giving, or arguments.

Apply your skills

Students could work in pairs to do this activity, discussing where and why they choose to break lines and change stanzas. It might be useful to do this on the computer, giving them the unformed block of text to play around with.

Share and compare the final poems that students come up with. Encourage them to alter or add to the words and images used in their poems, if they like.

Chapter 5 Vary sentences for clarity, purpose and effect

1 Vary your sentence lengths and structures

Getting you thinking

Read the extract from *The Old Curiosity Shop* with the class, emphasising the emotion. What are students' first thoughts about the passage? Once they have discussed in pairs the effect of the extract, help them to analyse why it is so effective: short sentences, repetitions, lists, question.

Apply your skills

Students should enjoy this extract from *The Haunted House*. Make sure they understand all the vocabulary. Ask them to say how clearly they can see the house in their minds' eyes. What details might they add? They should be able to produce effective writing of their own, following the guidelines.

2 Turn simple sentences into complex sentences

Getting you thinking

Read the first passage aloud to students, trying not to overemphasise the boring style! Ask for their reaction to it. Can they pinpoint why it's not exciting and attention-grabbing? Now read the second passage. Help them draw out what is better about it.

How does it work?

If students are not clear about simple and complex sentences, write on the board the first sentence from the first passage and the complex version of it from the second so that they can compare directly. Then write a few more simple sentences on the board and ask how to make them complex. Students can refer to the subordinating conjunctions in their books if necessary. Point out that conjunctions are particularly useful at the start of a sentence – to avoid repetition and to link it to the previous sentence.

Ask students whether they think the simple or complex sentences are more interesting. Explain that being able to vary the *length* and *word order* of sentences will make their writing more effective.

Apply your skills
After students have rewritten the passage in their own words, read the original passage from Conan Doyle's *Hound of the Baskervilles*. What do students think of it? How does it compare to their own versions?

3 Use subordinate clauses to add interest to your writing

Getting you thinking
Students may need a number of examples to help them understand the concept of a predicate. It is also worth making sure they understand the difference between a complex and a compound sentence.

How does it work?
Explain to students that 'who', 'whom' and 'whose' refer to people, while 'which' and 'that' refer to things.

As you move on to relative clauses, it will be helpful to give students lots of examples to illustrate how these clauses add information about people or things.

Apply your skills
As an extension, you could introduce *defining* and *non-defining* clauses. Give students the following two sentences:

The street that I live on is full of trees.

Some pupils at my school, which is in the next town, won the race last week.

In the first sentence, 'that I live on' is crucial to the meaning of the sentence. On the other hand, 'which is in the next town' is not important to understanding the second sentence: it merely adds detail.

4 Use connectives and vary the order of clauses in sentences

How does it work?
Encourage students to experiment with words. Following the example, can they come up with more sentences where they change the word order to put the emphasis on different parts? This is probably best done as a class, pooling ideas to create different effects. Students should then be able to work on the other activities in pairs.

Apply your skills
It would be helpful for students to do this activity on the computer, so they can edit sentences and move them around.

Encourage them to think about reordering the facts to increase their impact, as well as linking them together and changing the order of the sentences. Remind them that an attention-grabbing opening is vital. How would they achieve this?

5 Use different tenses for effect

How does it work?
Help students through the quite complex descriptions of verbs, and model for them how different tenses are formed and used. Make sure they know the difference between the present perfect (when something has happened in a past time period that extends to the present – today, this week, etc.) and the past perfect (something that happened in a time period that has completely finished – yesterday, last week).

You may also want to explain that agreement of subject and verb is very important.

- A *singular* subject must be matched to a singular verb form.
- A *plural* subject must have a plural verb form.

The following examples should help:

A group of us is calling for change.

Two *were* convicted (plural). None *was* to blame (singular).

Display this version:

A group of us are calling for change.

Explain that the 'us' has confused the writer. The singular subject is actually 'group', therefore the verb should be 'is'. This may also be a good opportunity to explain the difference between the subject and object of a verb: that subjects *carry out* the action and objects are *on the receiving end*.

I trapped the savage dog. The savage dog (subject) bit *me* (object).

Students frequently make mistakes with double subjects or objects:

My friend and me caught the bus home.

Dad gave John and I a lift to judo class.

Help them see the problem with these sentences by leaving out 'My friend' and 'John'. Would they say 'me caught' or 'Dad gave I'?

Apply your skills
This poem is excellent for making sure students understand what a present participle is! Encourage them to be as creative as possible when writing their own description, which could be prose or poetry.

Remind students that powerful writing is not always about using long lists of adjectives or adverbs. When they have to use more than one adverb, they should ask themselves: is there a stronger, more effective verb I could use here instead?

6 Use modal verbs for precision

Getting you thinking
Most of us use modal verbs confidently and without thinking. Some careless speech forms should be avoided: it is 'must have' or 'might have' not 'must of' or 'might of'.

Apply your skills
The letter might start in these ways:

Dear Dr Brown
My uncle and his family are visiting from Australia for the first time. I wonder if I might have one day…

Dear…
Thank you for your note. Family reunions are important but so are examinations. You ought not to…

> **Chapter 6   Write with technical accuracy of syntax and punctuation in phrases, clauses and sentences**

1 Use speech punctuation effectively

Getting you thinking
You could write the dialogue on the board without the punctuation and find out what the students know already. For example, do they know where the commas and question marks go?

Apply your skills
Encourage students to think about how the signalman reacted. What might the ghost want from him or be trying to tell him?

2 Use apostrophes for contractions in informal writing

Getting you thinking
Ensure students understand the difference between *it's*/*its* and *their*/*there*/*they're*.

Make sure they are clear that contractions should be used very carefully. They should be avoided in any formal writing, though they can be very effective in informal writing

How does it work?
Students may have noticed the number of contractions used in Shakespeare's plays.

3 Use apostrophes for possession

How does it work?
Work through the rules of the apostrophe for possession with the class and add more examples until they are clear about the rules. You could put a further 5–10 mixed examples on the board to consolidate students' learning.

Now you try it
Point out to students that explaining something to someone else is the surest way of checking you have really understood it yourself. This is why they are asked to work in pairs to check their answers and explain the rules. Take the opportunity to walk round and listen to their explanations.

4 Use semicolons accurately

Getting you thinking
You might want to look up the full version of this Dickens episode (*Barnaby Rudge* Chapter 55) to hear the drama and understand how the semicolons give slight pauses and breathing spaces.

Apply your skills
Rupert Brooke's poem offers an excellent example of the semicolon used in lists. Explain why he was reminiscing in this way about the things he loved in life. Point out that they can use commas, too, for lighter pauses or divisions in their list poem.

5 Use colons accurately

Getting you thinking
The more usual use of the colon (to introduce a list divided by semicolons) was touched on in the previous lesson.

Apply your skills
This activity reinforces the use of the colon but also offers students the opportunity to be more creative in their writing.

6 Use other forms of punctuation for effect

How does it work?
Explain to students that, whilst a dash can sometimes replace a colon (as in, 'I have worked in these charity shops – Oxfam, Save the Children and RSPCA'), it is generally better to use the colon in their school work.

Now you try it

Once students have reviewed their articles in pairs, ask them to read each other's version aloud. Does the punctuation help them to read it in the right tone of voice?

Apply your skills

As an extension activity students could find magazine articles, letters, reviews or blogs and identify the use of brackets, dashes or exclamation marks for effect in them.

Chapter 7   Select appropriate and effective vocabulary

1 Understand how words are constructed

Now you try it

To build on students' knowledge, a list of prefixes and suffixes could be made on the board (along with their meaning, origins and examples of use).

Apply your skills

To develop students' interest in how our language has been influenced by the language of other countries, a map could be given to students or put on the board, accompanied by a list of words. They could use dictionaries or the internet to work out where these words come from and then place them on the map. Example words might be:

amen, banana, bangle, brogues, bungalow, chutney, concert, diva, espresso, galore, geek, golf, hooligan, iceberg, jazz, jodhpurs, jubilee, jungle, karaoke, luck, marmalade, mosquito, opera, phoney, potato, pyjamas, safari, shampoo, slogan, tea, thug, tycoon, voodoo, walrus, water, wok, zombie.

2 Use precise vocabulary to make your ideas clearer

Getting you thinking

Read the two drafts aloud to the students, or ask for a volunteer to read them. Which do they prefer and why? How does each one make them feel? Elicit their ideas, then explain the difference between the two further if necessary, and find out from the students if they think she has succeeded.

Now you try it

Explain to students that their word choices will affect the sound and pace of a piece of writing. Choosing words that alliterate (start with the same letter) can have a powerful effect. They should try reading their revised passage aloud to test out the new tone and tempo they have created.

3 Choose vocabulary that is appropriate for your purpose

Getting you thinking

Read the first draft to the class. What do they think? Does it present a strong argument in favour of the use of mobile phones in the classroom? What could be done differently/better? Change some of the words on the board. Read the class's creation, then the second draft from the text. What do they think of this new draft?

Apply your skills

An extra task could be added on modal verbs. Begin by explaining that these are added to verbs to introduce a sense of likelihood, permission, necessity or ability. Then put the key modal verbs on the board (can, could, may, might, must, shall, should, will, would). Ask students to use them in a sentence, and to decide how the modal affects the sentence in terms of suggesting likelihood, permission, necessity or ability. Finally, discuss which ones would be particularly useful when advising someone about staying safe on the internet.

4 Make effective use of synonyms

Now you try it
If students are using a thesaurus, make sure they check their choice of words carefully.

You could have some fun illustrating the sort of mistakes that can be made!

Chapter 8   Use correct spelling

1 Spell words with prefixes correctly

Now you try it
During feedback, put together a long list on the board of all the prefixes that students have discovered. This could be used as a basis for a spelling test, or as a game (with students standing up and facing away from the board whilst you erase three or four words; selected students can then come up and rewrite them, with the correct spelling, on the board).

2 Spell words with suffixes correctly

Extension activity
In pairs, write the words from the list opposite on a big sheet of paper using three different coloured pens. Choose one colour for the prefixes, another colour for the suffixes and another colour for the words on the left. Then cut out the words to make small cards. Using the cards, see what new words you can create by adding a prefix or a suffix. Use a dictionary to check that your new words exist.

Words		Prefixes	Suffixes
fact	alter	re	able
love	mature	dis	ation
walk	hesitate	un	er
inform	grow	im	ion
do	charm	in	ing
play	spell	sub	less
worry	standard		
similar	wash		
exceptional	concoct		
clear	elect		

3 Spell homophones correctly

Extension activity
Work in groups of three or four. You are going to be playing against everyone else in the class on a timer. The group to come up with the most homophones in the time limit wins! Try to go right through the alphabet. Some letters are harder than others, although even the letters x and z share a homophone! For example:

ail	ale
bare	